ggplot2: Guide to Create Beautiful Graphics in R

Alboukadel Kassambara

0.1   Preface to the second edition

We have been gratified by the popularity of the first edition of *"ggplot2: the elements for elegant data visualization in R"*. This, along with the release of the version 2.0 of ggplot2 R package, motivated us to update our book with a second edition.

We have simplified several chapters, including quick plot, density plots, histogram plots, ECDF plots and QQ plots. We have added new chapters and updated some of the existing chapters. Here is a summary of the main changes:

1. **New features added**:

- Introduction to R (chapter 1)
- Area plot (chapter 3)
- Frequency polygon (chapter 7)
- Dot plot for one variable (chapter 8)
- Scatter plot (chapter 12)
    - quantile line from quantile regression
    - jitter to reduce overplotting
- Continuous bivariate distribution (chapter 13)
- Correlation Matrix Visualization (chapter 41)
    - ggcorrplot: new R package for visualizing a correlation matrix
- Line plot with time series data updated
- Graphical parameters:
    - Position adjustements (chapter 38)
    - Coordinate systems (chapter 39)
    - Text annotations: ggrepel R package (chapter 34)
- survminer: new R package for plotting survival curves with number at risk table (chapter 42)

2. **Removed sections**:

- Line plot
    - "Add arrow" section removed
- Legend
    - Section "remove legend slashes" (not required since ggplot2 v2)

0.2 Preface to the first edition

ggplot2 is an R package implemented by **Hadley Wickham** for creating graphs. It's based on the Grammar of Graphics, a concept published by **Leland Wilkinson** in 2005.

ggplot2 has become a popular package for data visualization. The official documentation of the package is available at: http://docs.ggplot2.org/current/. However, going through this comprehensive documentation can "drive you crazy"!

To make things easy and simple, we'll present, in this book, the most important functions available in ggplot2 package to generate nice looking graphs. You will find many examples of R codes and graphics in this document.

Note that, all the analyses in this book were performed using R (ver. 3.2.3) and ggplot2 (ver 2.1.0).

0.3 Acknowledgments

- Thanks to Leland Wilkinson for the concept,
- Thanks to Hadley Wickham for ggplot2 R package

0.4 About the author

Alboukadel Kassambara is a PhD in Bioinformatics and Cancer Biology. He works since many years on genomic data analysis and visualization. He created a bioinformatics tool named GenomicScape (www.genomicscape.com) which is an easy-to-use web tool for gene expression data analysis and visualization. He developed also a website called STHDA (Statistical Tools for High-throughput Data Analysis, www.sthda.com), which contains many tutorials on data analysis and visualization using R software and packages. He is the author of the R packages **survminer** (for analyzing and drawing survival curves), **ggcorrplot** (for drawing correlation matrix using ggplot2) and **factoextra** (to easily extract and visualize the results of multivariate analysis such PCA, CA, MCA and clustering).

Contents

0.5   How this book is organized?

This book contains 6 parts. The first part provides a **quick introduction to R** (chapter 1) and to **ggplot2 plotting system** (chapter 2).

In the second part (chapter 3 - 11), we described the different graphs for **visualizing one continous/discrete variable**: area plots, density plots, histogram plots, frequency polygon, dot plots, ECDF and QQ plots.

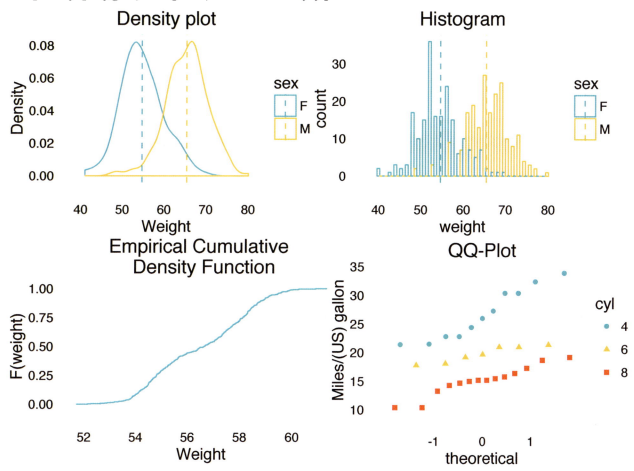

Part III provides quick-start guides for **plotting two continuous/discretes variables**, including :

- Scatter plots (chapter 12)
- Continuous bivariate distribution (chapter 13)
- Jitter plots of two discretes variables (chapter 14)

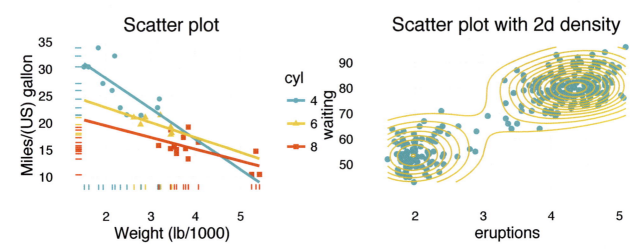

Part IV (chapter 15 - 22) describes how to draw and customize: box plots, violin plots, dot plots, strip charts, line plots, bar plots and pie charts.

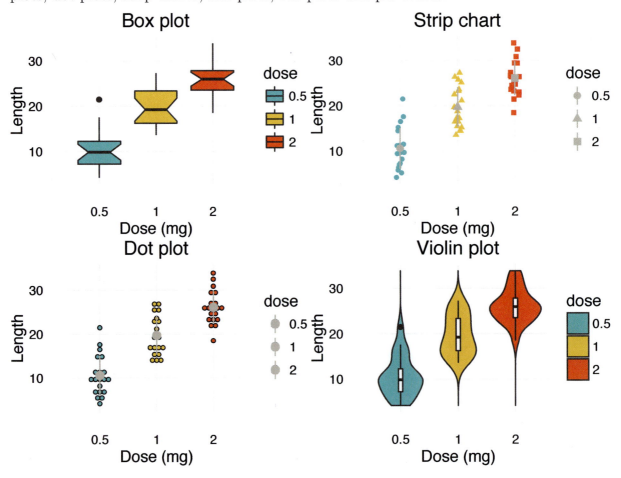

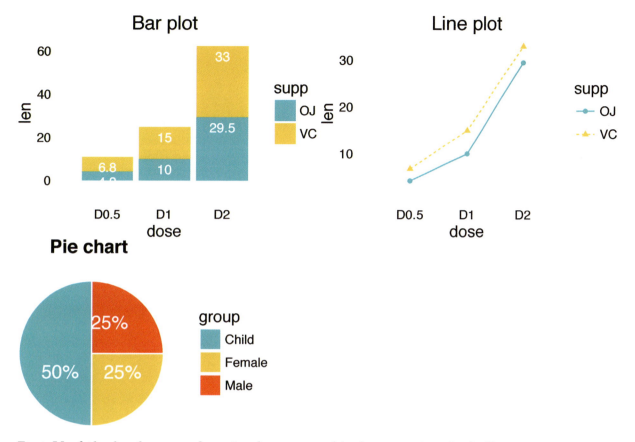

Part V of the book covers how to change graphical parameters including:

- Main title, axis labels and legend titles (chapter 24)
- Legend position and appearance (chapter 25)
- Colors (chapter 26)
- Point shapes, colors and size (chapter 27)
- Line types (chapter 28)
- Axis limits: minimum and maximum values (chapter 29)
- Axis transformations: log and sqrt (chapter 30)
- Date axes (chapter 31)
- Axis ticks : customize tick marks and labels (chapter 32)
- Themes and background colors (chapter 33)
- Add text annotations to a graph (chapter 34)
- Add straight lines to a plot: horizontal, vertical and regression lines (chapter 35)
- Rotate a plot (chapter 36)
- Facets: split a plot into a matrix of panels (chapter 37)
- Position adjustments (chapter 38)

- Coordinate systems (chapter)

Part VI describes some extensions of ggplot2 including:

- Arranging multiple graphs on the same page (chapter)
- Correlation matrix visualization (chapter)
- Plotting survival curves (chapter)

Survival curves and correlation matrix:

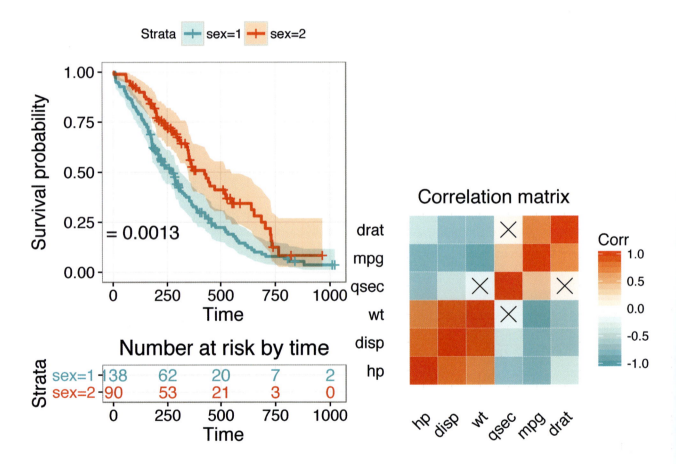

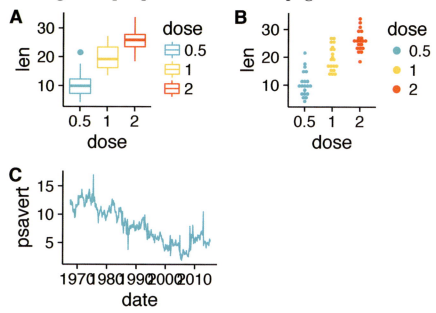

Each chapter is organized as an independent quick start guide. This means that, you don't need to read the different chapters in sequence. I just recommend to read firstly the chapter 1, as it gives a quick overview of R and ggplot2 graphing system.

For each chapter, the covered ggplot2 key functions are generally mentioned at the beginning. The used data are described and many examples of R codes and graphics are provided.

Sometimes, different chapters use the same data. In this case, we decided to repeat the data preparation description in the corresponding chapters. In other words, each chapter is an independent module and this gives the possibility to the user to read only the chapter of interest.

0.6   Book website

The website for this book is located at : http://www.sthda.com/english/wiki/ggplot2-essentials. It contains number of ressources.

0.7 How to execute the R codes provided in this book?

For a single line R code, you can just copy the code from the PDF to the R console.

For a multiple-line R codes, an error is generated, sometimes, when you copy and paste directly the R code from the PDF to the R console. If this happens, a solution is to:

- Paste firstly the code in your R code editor or in your text editor
- Copy the code from your text/code editor to the R console

Part I

Basics of R and ggplot2

Chapter 1

Introduction to R

R is a free and powerful statistical software for **analyzing** and **visualizing** data. If you want to learn easily the essential of R programming, visit our series of tutorials available on STHDA: http://www.sthda.com/english/wiki/r-basics-quick-and-easy.

In this chapter, we provide a very brief introduction to **R**, for installing R/RStudio as well as importing your data into R.

1.1 Install R and RStudio

R and RStudio can be installed on Windows, MAC OSX and Linux platforms. RStudio is an integrated development environment for R that makes using R easier. It includes a console, code editor and tools for plotting.

1. R can be downloaded and installed from the Comprehensive R Archive Network (CRAN) webpage (http://cran.r-project.org/).

2. After installing R software, install also the RStudio software available at: http://www.rstudio.com/products/RStudio/.

3. Launch RStudio and start use R inside R studio.

RStudio screen:

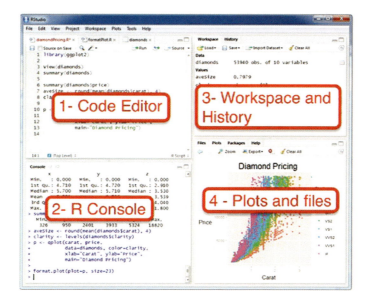

1.2 Arithmetics with R

- **Basic arithmetic operations**: + (addition), - (subtraction), * (multiplication), / (division), ^ (exponentiation)

Type this in R console:

```
7 + 4 # => 11
7 - 4 # => 3
7 / 2 # => 3.5
7 * 2 # => 14
```

- **Basic arithmetic functions**:
  - Logarithms and exponentials: **log2**(x), **log10**(x), **exp**(x)
  - Other mathematical functions: **abs**(x): absolute value; **sqrt**(x): square root.

```
log2(4) # => 2
abs(-4) # => 4
sqrt(4) # => 2
```

1.3   Data types in R

- **Basic data types**: **numeric**, **character** and **logical**

```
my_age <- 28 # Numeric variable
my_name <- "Nicolas" # Character variable
#  Are you a data scientist?: (yes/no) <=> (TRUE/FALSE)
is_datascientist <- TRUE # logical variable
```

- **Vectors**: a combination of multiple values (numeric, character or logical)
  - Create a vector: **c**() for concatenate
  - Get a subset of a vector: my_vector[i] to get the ith element
  - Calculations with vectors: **max**(x), **min**(x), **length**(x), **sum**(x), **mean**(x), **sd**(x): standard deviation, **var**(x): variance.

```
# Create a numeric vector
friend_ages <- c(27, 25, 29, 26)
mean(friend_ages) # => 26.75
max(friend_ages) # => 29
friend_ages[2] # age of my friends number 2 => 25
```

- **Matrices**: like an Excel sheet containing multiple rows and columns. Combination of multiple vectors with the same types (numeric, character or logical).
  - Create and naming matrix: **matrix**(), **cbind**(), **rbind**(), **rownames**(x), **colnames**(x)
  - Convert x to a matrix: x2 <- **as.matrix**(x)
  - Dimensions of a matrix: **ncol**(x), **nrow**(x), **dim**(x)
  - Get a subset of a matrix: my_data[row, col]
  - Calculations with numeric matrices: **rowSums**(x), **colSums**(x), **rowMeans**(x), **colMeans**(x)

```
# Numeric vectors
col1 <- c(5, 6, 7, 8, 9)
col2 <- c(2, 4, 5, 9, 8)
```

```
col3 <- c(7, 3, 4, 8, 7)
# Combine the vectors by column
my_data <- cbind(col1, col2, col3)
# Change rownames
rownames(my_data) <- c("row1", "row2", "row3", "row4", "row5")
my_data
```

```
##      col1 col2 col3
## row1    5    2    7
## row2    6    4    3
## row3    7    5    4
## row4    8    9    8
## row5    9    8    7
```

- **Factors**: grouping variables in your data
    - Create a factor: **factor**()
    - Convert x to a factor: x2 <- **as.factor**(x)
    - Calculations with factors:
        * Number of elements in each category: **summary**(x), **table**(x)
        * Compute some statistics by groups (for example, mean by groups): **tapply**()

```
# Create a factor
friend_groups <- factor(c("grp1", "grp2", "grp1", "grp2"))
levels(friend_groups) # => "grp1", "grp2"
```

```
## [1] "grp1" "grp2"
```

```
# Compute the mean age by groups
friend_ages <- c(27, 25, 29, 26)
tapply(friend_ages, friend_groups, mean)
```

```
## grp1 grp2
## 28.0 25.5
```

- **Data frames**: like a matrix but can have columns with different types
    - Create a data frame: **data.frame**()
    - Convert x to a data frame: x2 <- **as.data.frame**(x)
    - Subset a data frame: my_data[row, col]

```
# Create a data frame
friends_data <- data.frame(
  name = c("Nicolas", "Thierry", "Bernard", "Jerome"),
  age = c(27, 25, 29, 26) ,
  height = c(180, 170, 185, 169),
  married = c(TRUE, FALSE, TRUE, TRUE)
)
friends_data
```

```
##        name age height married
## 1 Nicolas  27     180    TRUE
## 2 Thierry  25     170   FALSE
## 3 Bernard  29     185    TRUE
## 4  Jerome  26     169    TRUE
```

Read more at: http://www.sthda.com/english/wiki/easy-r-programming-basics

1.4   Getting help with functions in R

If you want to learn more about a given function, say **mean**(), type this:

```
?mean
```

1.5   Installing and loading R packages

An **R package** is an extension of R containing data sets and specific R functions to solve specific questions.

For example, in this book, you'll learn how to draw beautiful graphs using the **ggplot2** R package.

There are thousands other R packages available for download and installation from CRAN, Bioconductor(biology related R packages) and GitHub repositories.

1. How to install packages from CRAN? Use the function **install.packages**():

```r
# ggplot2: for data visualization
install.packages("ggplot2")

# dplyr: for data manipulation
install.packages("dplyr")
```

2. How to install packages from GitHub? You should first install **devtools** if you don't have it already installed on your computer:

For example, the following R code installs the latest version of **survminer** R package developed by A. Kassambara (https://github.com/kassambara/survminer).

```r
install.packages("devtools")
devtools::install_github("kassambara/survminer")
```

Note that, GitHub contains the developmental version of R packages.

3. After installation, you must first load the package for using the functions in the package. The function **library**() is used for this task.

```r
library("ggplot2")
```

Now, we can use ggplot2 functions for drawing elegant graphs.

1.6   Importing your data into R

1. **Prepare your file** as follow:

   - Use the first row as **column names**. Generally, columns represent **variables**
   - Use the first column as **row names**. Generally rows represent **observations**.
   - Each row/column name should be unique, so remove duplicated names.
   - Avoid names with blank spaces. Good column names: *Long_jump* or *Long.jump*. Bad column name: *Long jump*.
   - Avoid names with special symbols: ?, $, *, +, #, (,), -, /, }, {, |, >, < etc. Only underscore can be used.
   - Avoid beginning variable names with a number. Use letter instead. Good column names: sport_100m or x100m. Bad column name: 100m
   - R is case sensitive. This means that Name is different from Name or NAME.
   - Avoid blank rows in your data
   - Delete any comments in your file
   - Replace missing values by **NA** (for not available)
   - If you have a column containing date, use the four digit format. Good format: 01/01/2016. Bad format: 01/01/16

2. Our **finale file** should look like this:

3. **Save your file**

We recommend to save your file into **.txt** (tab-delimited text file) or **.csv** (comma separated value file) format.

4. **Get your data into R**:

Use the R code below. You will be asked to choose a file:

```
# .txt file: Read tab separated values
my_data <- read.delim(file.choose())

# .csv file: Read comma (",") separated values
my_data <- read.csv(file.choose())

# .csv file: Read semicolon (";") separated values
my_data <- read.csv2(file.choose())
```

You can read more about how to import data into R at this link:
http://www.sthda.com/english/wiki/importing-data-into-r

1.7 Demo data sets

R comes with several **built-in data sets**, which are generally used as demo data for playing with R functions.

The most used R demo data sets include: **mtcars**, **iris**, **ToothGrowth** and **Plant-Growth**. To load a demo data set, use the function **data()** as follow:

```
# Loading
data(mtcars)

# Print the first 3 rows
head(mtcars, 3)
```

```
##                   mpg cyl disp  hp drat    wt  qsec vs am gear carb
## Mazda RX4         21.0   6  160 110 3.90 2.620 16.46  0  1    4    4
## Mazda RX4 Wag     21.0   6  160 110 3.90 2.875 17.02  0  1    4    4
## Datsun 710        22.8   4  108  93 3.85 2.320 18.61  1  1    4    1
```

If you want learn more about mtcars data sets, type this:

```
?mtcars
```

> mtcars data set is an object of class **data frame**.

To select just certain columns from a data frame, you can either refer to the columns by name or by their location (i.e., column 1, 2, 3, etc.).

```
# Access the data in 'mpg' column
# dollar sign is used
mtcars$mpg
```

```
##  [1] 21.0 21.0 22.8 21.4 18.7 18.1 14.3 24.4 22.8 19.2 17.8 16.4 17.3 15.2
## [15] 10.4 10.4 14.7 32.4 30.4 33.9 21.5 15.5 15.2 13.3 19.2 27.3 26.0 30.4
## [29] 15.8 19.7 15.0 21.4
```

```
# Or use this
mtcars[, 'mpg']
```

1.8   Close your R/RStudio session

Each time you close R/RStudio, you will be asked whether you want to save the data from your R session. If you decide to save, the data will be available in future R sessions.

Chapter 2

Introduction to ggplot2

2.1 What's ggplot2?

ggplot2 is a powerful and a flexible **R package**, implemented by **Hadley Wickham**, for producing elegant graphics. The **gg** in ggplot2 means **Grammar of Graphics**, a graphic concept which describes plots by using a "grammar".

> According to ggplot2 concept, a plot can be divided into different fundamental parts : **Plot = data + Aesthetics + Geometry**.

data: is a data frame

Aesthetics: is used to indicate x and y variables. It can be also used to control the **color**, the **size** or the **shape** of points, the height of bars, etc.....

Geometry: corresponds to the type of graphics (**histogram, box plot, line plot, density plot, dot plot**, ...)

Two main functions, for creating plots, are available in **ggplot2** package :

qplot(): A quick plot function which is easy to use for simple plots.

ggplot(): A more flexible and robust function than **qplot** for building a plot piece by piece.

The output plot can be kept as a variable and then printed at any time using the function **print**()

After creating plots, two other important functions are:

last_plot(): returns the last plot to be modified

ggsave("plot.png", width = 5, height = 5): saves the last plot in the current working directory.

This document describes how to create and customize different types of graphs using ggplot2. Many examples of code and graphics are provided.

2.2   Type of graphs for data visualization

The type of plots, to be created, depends on the format of your data. The ggplot2 package provides methods for visualizing the following data structures:

1. **One variable - x**: continuous or discrete

2. **Two variables - x & y**: continuous and/or discrete

3. **Continuous bivariate distribution - x & y** (both continuous)

4. **Continuous function**

5. **Error bar**

6. **Maps**

7. **Three variables**

In the current document we'll provide the essential ggplot2 functions for drawing each of these seven data formats.

2.3   Install and load ggplot2 package

Use the **R** code below to install the latest version:

```r
# Installation
install.packages('ggplot2')

# Loading
library(ggplot2)
```

2.4   Data format and preparation

> The data must be a **data.frame** that contains all the information to make a ggplot. In the data, columns should be variables and rows should be observations).

We'll use the **mtcars** data set as an example of data:

```r
# Load the data
data(mtcars)
df <- mtcars[, c("mpg", "cyl", "wt")]

# Convert cyl to a factor variable
df$cyl <- as.factor(df$cyl)

# Print a sample of the data
head(df)
```

```
##                    mpg cyl    wt
## Mazda RX4          21.0   6 2.620
## Mazda RX4 Wag      21.0   6 2.875
## Datsun 710         22.8   4 2.320
## Hornet 4 Drive     21.4   6 3.215
## Hornet Sportabout  18.7   8 3.440
## Valiant            18.1   6 3.460
```

2.5   qplot() function: Draw quick plots

The **qplot()** function is very similar to the standard **R** base **plot()** function. It can be used to create quickly and easily different types of graphs: **scatter plots**, **box plots**, **violin plots**, **histogram** and **density plots**.

A simplified format of **qplot()** is :

```r
qplot(x, y = NULL, data, geom="auto")
```

- **x, y** : x and y values, respectively. The argument y is optional depending on the type of graphs to be created.

- **data** : data frame to use (optional).

- **geom** : Character vector specifying geom to use. Defaults to "point" if x and y are specified, and "histogram" if only x is specified.

Other arguments such as *main, xlab* and *ylab* can be also used to add main title and axis labels to the plot.

2.5.1   Scatter plots

The R code below creates basic **scatter plots** using the argument **geom = "point"**. It's also possible to combine different geoms (e.g.: **geom = c("point", "smooth")**, or **geom = c("point", "text")**).

```r
# Load data
data(mtcars)
# Basic scatter plot
qplot(x = mpg, y = wt, data = mtcars, geom = "point")

# Scatter plot with smoothed line
qplot(mpg, wt, data = mtcars,
      geom = c("point", "smooth"))
```

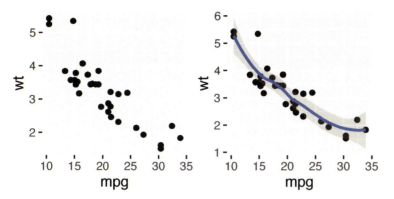

The following R code will change the **color** and the **shape** of points by groups. The column *cyl* will be used as grouping variable. In other words, the color and the shape of points will be changed by the levels of *cyl*.

```r
# Change the color by a continuous numeric variable
qplot(mpg, wt, data = mtcars, color = cyl)
```

```r
# Change color and shape by groups (factor)
mtcars$cyl <- factor(mtcars$cyl)
qplot(mpg, wt, data = mtcars, colour = cyl, shape = cyl)
```

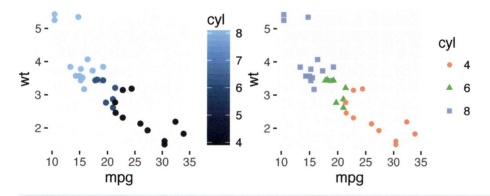

Like color, the **shape** and the **size** of points can be controlled by a continuous or discrete variable.

```r
# Change the size of points according to
  # the values of a continuous variable
qplot(mpg, wt, data = mtcars, size = mpg)
```

2.5.2   Box plot, histogram and density plots

The R code below generates some data containing the weights by sex (M for male; F for female):

```r
set.seed(1234)
wdata = data.frame(
        sex = factor(rep(c("F", "M"), each=200)),
        weight = c(rnorm(200, 55), rnorm(200, 58)))
head(wdata, 3)
```

```
##   sex   weight
## 1   F 53.79293
## 2   F 55.27743
## 3   F 56.08444
```

```r
# Basic box plot from data frame
# Change fill color by sex
qplot(sex, weight, data = wdata,
      geom = "boxplot")

# Basic histogram
qplot(weight, data = wdata, geom = "histogram")

# Density plot with main titles and axis labels
qplot(weight, data = wdata, geom = "density",
      xlab = "Weight (kg)", ylab = "Density",
      main = "Density plot")
```

2.6 ggplot() function: Build plots piece by piece

As mentioned above, the function **ggplot**() is powerful and more flexible than **qplot**(). This section describes briefly how to use **ggplot()** to build piece by piece an elegant plot.

Recall that, the concept of **ggplot** divides a plot into three different fundamental parts: **plot = data + Aesthetics + geometry**.

To demonstrate how the function **ggplot()** works, we'll draw a **scatter plot**. The function **aes**() is used to specify x and y variables as well as aesthetics (e.g., color, shape, size). An alternative option is the function **aes_string**() which, generates mappings from a string.

```
# Basic scatter plot
ggplot(data = mtcars, aes(x = wt, y = mpg)) +
  geom_point()
```

```
# Change the point size, and shape
ggplot(mtcars, aes(x = wt, y = mpg)) +
  geom_point(size = 1.5, shape = 18)
```

The function **aes_string**() can be used as follow:

```
ggplot(mtcars, aes_string(x = "wt", y = "mpg")) +
  geom_point(size = 2, shape = 23)
```

Note that, some plots visualize a **transformation** of the original data set. In this case, an alternative way to build a layer is to use **stat_*()** functions.

In the following example, the function **geom__density()** does the same as the function **stat__density()**:

```
# Use geometry function
ggplot(wdata, aes(x = weight)) + geom_density()

# OR use stat function
ggplot(wdata, aes(x = weight)) + stat_density()
```

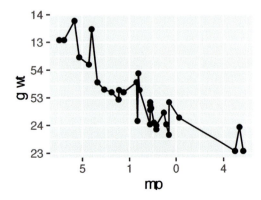

For each plot type, we'll provide the **geom__*()** function and the corresponding **stat__*()** function (if available).

In ggplot2 terminology, the functions **geom_point()** and **geom_density()** are called layers. You can combine multiple layers as follow:

```
ggplot(data = mtcars, aes(x = wt, y = mpg)) +
  geom_point() + # to draw points
  geom_line() # to draw a line
```

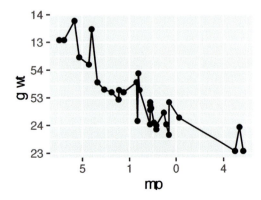

In the R code above, the two layers, **geom_point()** and **geom_line()**, use the same data and the same aesthetic mapping provided in the main function **ggplot**.

Note that, it's possible to use different data and mapping for different layers.

For example in the R code below:

- The entire *mtcars* data is used by the layer *geom_point()*
- A subset of *mtcars* data is used by the layer *geom_line()*. The line is colored according to the values of the continuous variable *cyl*.

```
ggplot(data = mtcars, aes(x = wt, y = mpg)) +
  geom_point() + # to draw points
  geom_line(data = head(mtcars), color = "red")
```

It's also possible to do simple calculations in the function **aes()**.

```
# Log2 transformation in the aes()
ggplot(data = mtcars, aes(x = log2(wt), y = log2(mpg))) +
  geom_point()
```

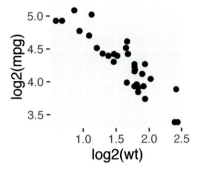

As mentioned above, the function **aes_string()** is used for aesthetic mappings from string objects. An example is shown below:

```
ggplot(data = mtcars, aes_string(x = "wt", y = "mpg")) +
  geom_point(color = "red") +
  geom_smooth()
```

> Note that, **aes_string()** is particularly useful when writing functions that create plots because you can use strings to define the aesthetic mappings, rather than having to use substitute to generate a call to **aes()** (see the R function below).

```
# Helper function for creating a scatter plot
# +++++++++++++++++++++
# data: data frame
# xName,yName: specify x and y variables, respectively
ggpoints <- function (data, xName, yName){
  p <- ggplot(data = data, aes_string(xName, yName)) +
    geom_point(color = "red") +
    geom_smooth()

  return(p)
}
```

Create a scatter plot using the helper function **ggpoints()**:

```
ggpoints(mtcars, xName ="wt", yName = "mpg")
```

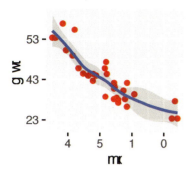

2.7 Save ggplots

To print directly a ggplot to a file, the function **print()** is used:

```
# Print the plot to a pdf file
pdf("myplot.pdf")
myplot <- ggplot(mtcars, aes(wt, mpg)) + geom_point()
print(myplot)
dev.off()
```

For printing to a **png** file, use:

```
png("myplot.png")
print(myplot)
dev.off()
```

It's also possible to make a ggplot and to save it from the screen using the function **ggsave()**:

```
# 1. Create a plot: displayed on the screen (by default)
ggplot(mtcars, aes(wt, mpg)) + geom_point()
# 2.1. Save the plot to a pdf
ggsave("myplot.pdf")
# 2.2 OR save it to png file
ggsave("myplot.png")
```

Part II

Plot One Variable - X: Continuous or Discrete

2.8 Data format

The R code below generates some data (**wdata**) containing the weights by sex (M for male; F for female):

```
set.seed(1234)
wdata = data.frame(
        sex = factor(rep(c("F", "M"), each=200)),
        weight = c(rnorm(200, 55), rnorm(200, 58)))

head(wdata, 4)
```

```
##   sex   weight
## 1   F 53.79293
## 2   F 55.27743
## 3   F 56.08444
## 4   F 52.65430
```

The following R code computes the mean value by "sex", using dplyr package. First, the data is grouped by sex and then summarised by computing the mean weight by groups. The operator %>% is used to combine multiple operations:

```
library("dplyr")
mu <- wdata %>%
  group_by(sex) %>%
  summarise(grp.mean = mean(weight))

head(mu)
```

```
## Source: local data frame [2 x 2]
##
##      sex grp.mean
##    (fctr)    (dbl)
## 1       F 54.94224
## 2       M 58.07325
```

In the next sections, the data **mu** we'll be used for adding mean line on the plots.

2.9 Plot types

We start by creating a plot, named **a**, that we'll finish in the next section by adding a layer.

```
a <- ggplot(wdata, aes(x = weight))
```

Possible layers are:

- For **one continuous variable**:
  - **geom_area**() for *area plot*
  - **geom_density**() for *density plot*
  - **geom_dotplot**() for *dot plot*
  - **geom_freqpoly**() for *frequency polygon*
  - **geom_histogram**() for *histogram plot*
  - **stat_ecdf**() for *empirical cumulative density function*
  - **stat_qq**() for *quantile - quantile plot*

- For **one discrete variable**:
  - **geom_bar**() for *bar plot*

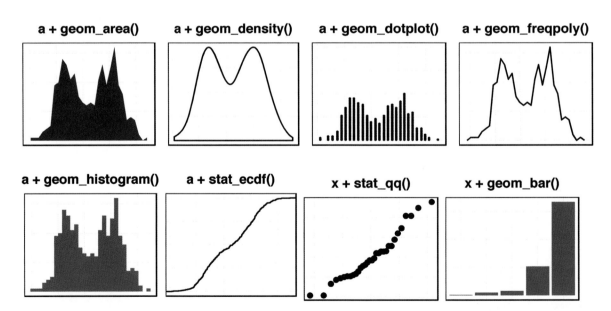

Chapter 3

Area Plots

An area plot is the continuous analog of a stacked bar chart (see Chapter 20).

- **Key function**: *geom_area()*

- **Alternative function**: *stat_bin()*

- **Key arguments to customize the plot**: *alpha, color, fill, linetype, size*

```
# Basic plot
# Change line and fill colors
a + geom_area(stat = "bin",
              color= "black", fill="#00AFBB")
```

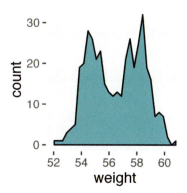

> Note that, by default y axis corresponds to the *count* of weight values. If you want to change the plot in order to have the *density* on y axis, the R code would be as follow.

```r
a + geom_area(aes(y = ..density..), stat ="bin")
```

The following plots compares bar plots and area plots. The *diamonds* data set [in **ggplot2** package] is used.

```r
# Load the data
data("diamonds")
p <- ggplot(diamonds, aes(x = price, fill = cut))

# Bar plot
p + geom_bar(stat = "bin")

# Area plot
p + geom_area(stat = "bin")
```

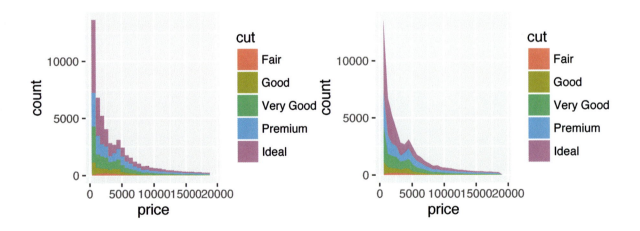

Chapter 4

Density Plots

A kernel density estimate is useful for visualizing the distribution of a continuous variable. The function **geom_density()** is used to create a **density plot**. You can also add a line for the mean using the function **geom_vline()** [Chapter 35]

- **Key function**: *geom_density()*

- **Alternative function**: *stat_density()*

- **Key arguments to customize the plot**: *alpha, color, fill, linetype, size*

4.1 Basic density plots

```
# Basic plot
a + geom_density()

# Change line color and fill color, add mean line
a + geom_density(color = "black", fill = "gray")+
  geom_vline(aes(xintercept=mean(weight)),
          color="#FC4E07", linetype="dashed", size=1)
```

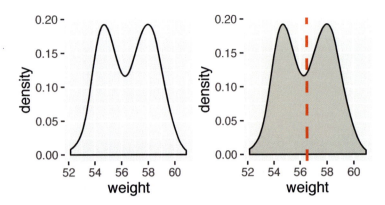

4.2   Change colors by groups

Density plot line and fill colors can be automatically controlled by the levels of *sex*:

```
# Change line colors by sex
a + geom_density(aes(color = sex))

# Change fill color by sex
# Use semi-transparent fill: alpha = 0.4
a + geom_density(aes(fill = sex), alpha=0.4)

# Add mean lines and color by sex
a + geom_density(aes(color = sex), alpha=0.4)+
  geom_vline(data = mu, aes(xintercept = grp.mean, color=sex),
             linetype="dashed")
```

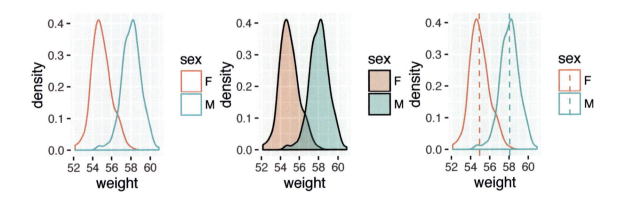

Change manually density plot line/fill colors using the functions :

- *scale_color_manual(), scale_fill_manual()* : to use custom colors
- *scale_color_brewer(), scale_fill_brewer()* : to use color palettes from *RColor-Brewer* package
- *scale_color_grey(), scale_fill_grey()* : to use grey color palettes

Change manually line colors:

```
# Add mean line and color manually
a2 <- a + geom_density(aes(color = sex)) +
    geom_vline(data = mu, aes(xintercept = grp.mean, color = sex),
               linetype="dashed") + theme_minimal()
a2 + scale_color_manual(values=c("#999999", "#E69F00"))

# Use brewer color palettes
a2 + scale_color_brewer(palette="Paired")

# Use grey scale
a2 + scale_color_grey()
```

Change manually fill colors:

```
# Fill manually
a3 <- a + geom_density(aes(fill = sex), alpha = 0.4) + theme_minimal()
a3 + scale_fill_manual(values=c("#999999", "#E69F00"))

# Use brewer color palettes
a3 + scale_fill_brewer(palette="Dark2") + theme_minimal()

# Use grey scale
a3 + scale_fill_grey() + theme_minimal()
```

Read more on ggplot2 colors here: Chapter 26

Chapter 5

Histogram Plots

A Histogram represents the distribution of a continuous variable by dividing into bins and counting the number of observations in each bin. The function **geom_histogram()** is used to create a **histogram plot**. You can also add a line for the mean using the function **geom_vline()** [Chapter 35].

- **Key function**: *geom_histogram()*

- **Alternative functions**: *stat_bin()*

- **Position adjustments**: "identity" (or *position_identity()*), "stack" (or *position_stack()*), "dodge" (or *position_dodge()*). Default value is "stack"

- **Key arguments to customize the plot**: *alpha, color, fill, linetype, size*

5.1   Basic histogram plots

```
# Basic plot
a + geom_histogram()

# Change the number of bins
a + geom_histogram(bins = 50)

# Change line color and fill color, add mean line
a + geom_histogram(color = "black", fill = "gray")+
  geom_vline(aes(xintercept=mean(weight)),
          color="#FC4E07", linetype="dashed", size=1)
```

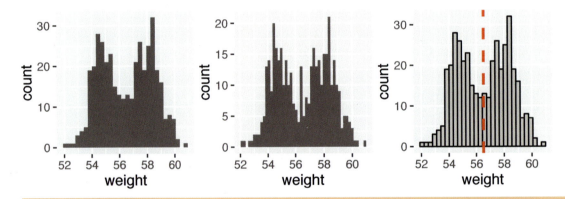

> Note that by default, **stat_bin** uses 30 bins - this might not be good default. You can change the number of bins (**e.g.: bins = 50** or the bin width **e.g.: binwidth = 0.5**.

> By default y axis corresponds to the *count* of weight values. If you want to change the plot in order to have the *density* on y axis, the R code would be as follow.

```
a + geom_histogram(aes(y = ..density..))
```

5.2 Change colors by groups

Histogram plot line colors can be automatically controlled by the levels of the variable *sex*.

> You can change the position adjustment to use for overlapping points on the layer. Possible values for the argument **position** are "identity", "stack", "dodge". Default value is "stack".

```r
# Change line colors by sex
a + geom_histogram(aes(color = sex), fill = "white")

# Position adjustment: "identity" (overlaid)
a + geom_histogram(aes(color = sex), fill = "white", alpha = 0.6,
                   position="identity")

# Position adjustment: "dodge" (Interleaved)
# Add mean lines and color by sex
a + geom_histogram(aes(color = sex), fill = "white",
                   position="dodge") +
    geom_vline(data = mu, aes(xintercept = grp.mean, color=sex),
               linetype="dashed")
```

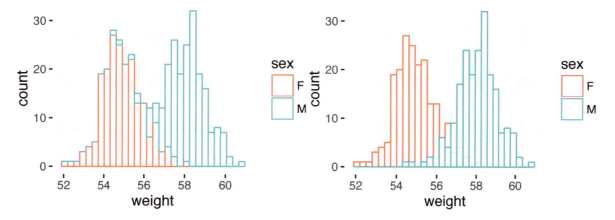

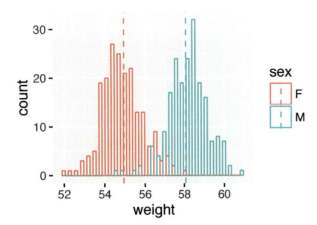

As described in the density plot chapter (Chapter 4), line and fill colors can be changed manually as follow:

```
# Use classic theme and change legend position to "top"
# Change outline color manually
a + geom_histogram(aes(color = sex), fill = "white",
                       alpha = 0.4, position = "identity") +
  scale_color_manual(values=c("#00AFBB", "#E7B800"))

# change fill and outline color manually
a + geom_histogram(aes(color = sex, fill = sex),
                       alpha = 0.4, position = "identity") +
  scale_fill_manual(values=c("#00AFBB", "#E7B800")) +
  scale_color_manual(values=c("#00AFBB", "#E7B800"))
```

Read more on ggplot2 colors here: Chapter 26

Chapter 6

Combine Histogram and Density Plots

- Plot histogram with density values on y-axis (instead of count values).
- Add density plot with transparent density plot

```r
# Histogram with density plot
a + geom_histogram(aes(y=..density..), colour="black", fill="white") +
 geom_density(alpha=0.2, fill = "#FF6666")

# Color by groups
a + geom_histogram(aes(y=..density.., color = sex, fill = sex),
                   alpha=0.5, position="identity")+
 geom_density(aes(color = sex), size = 1)
```

Chapter 7

Frequency Polygon

Frequency polygon is very close to histogram plots (Chapter: 5). It can be also used to visualize the distribution of a continuous variable. The difference between histograms and frequency polygon is that:

- Histograms use bars
- Frequency polygons use lines.

The function **geom_freqpoly()** is used to create a **frequency polygon**.

- **Key function**: *geom_freqpoly()*

- **Alternative functions**: *stat_bin()*

- **Key arguments to customize the plot**: *alpha, color, linetype, size*

```
# Basic plot
a + geom_freqpoly(bins = 30) +
  theme_minimal()


# Change color and linetype by sex
# Use custom color palettes
a + geom_freqpoly(aes(color = sex, linetype = sex))+
  scale_color_manual(values=c("#999999", "#E69F00"))+
   theme_minimal()
```

If you want to change the plot in order to have the *density* on y axis, the R code would be as follow.

```
a + geom_freqpoly(aes(y = ..density..))
```

Chapter 8

Dot Plots for One Variable

In a **dot plot**, dots are stacked with each dot representing one observation. The width of a dot corresponds to the bin width.

- **Key function**: *geom_dotplot()*

- **Key arguments to customize the plot**: *alpha, color, fill and dotsize*

```
# change fill and color by sex
a + geom_dotplot(aes(fill = sex))
```

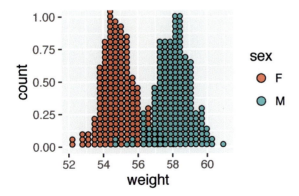

Chapter 9

ECDF Plots

ECDF (Empirical Cumulative Density Function) reports for any given number the percent of individuals that are below that threshold.

- **Key function**: *stat_ecdf()*

- **Key arguments to customize the plot**: *alpha, color, linetype and size*

```
a + stat_ecdf(geom = "point")
a + stat_ecdf(geom = "step")
```

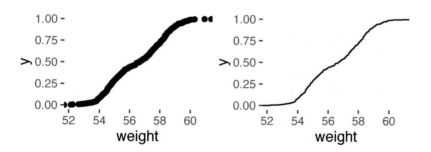

For any value, say, height = 50, you can see that about 25% of our individuals are shorter than 50 inches.

Chapter 10

QQ Plots

QQ-plots (or Quantile - Quantile plots) are used to check whether a given data follows *normal distribution*. The function **stat_qq()** or **qplot()** can be used to create qq-plots.

- **Key function**: *stat_qq()*

- **Key arguments to customize the plot**: *alpha, color, shape and size*

- *mtcars* data sets are used in the examples below.

```
data(mtcars)
# Convert cyl column from a numeric to a factor variable
mtcars$cyl <- as.factor(mtcars$cyl)
head(mtcars[, c("mpg", "cyl")])
```

```
##                    mpg cyl
## Mazda RX4          21.0   6
## Mazda RX4 Wag      21.0   6
## Datsun 710         22.8   4
## Hornet 4 Drive     21.4   6
## Hornet Sportabout 18.7   8
## Valiant            18.1   6
```

- Create qq plots

```r
p <- ggplot(mtcars, aes(sample=mpg))

# Basic plot
p + stat_qq()


# Change point shapes by groups
# Use custom color palettes
p + stat_qq(aes(shape = cyl, color = cyl))+
  scale_color_manual(values=c("#00AFBB", "#E7B800", "#FC4E07"))
```

Read more on ggplot2 colors here: Chapter 26

Chapter 11

Bar Plots of Counts

The function **geom_bar()** can be used to visualize one discrete variable. In this case, the count of each level is plotted.

- **Key function**: *geom_bar()*

- **Alternative function**: *stat_count()*

- **Key arguments to customize the plot**: *alpha, color, fill, linetype and size*

We'll use the **mpg** data set [in **ggplot2** package]. The R code is as follow:

```r
data(mpg)
ggplot(mpg, aes(fl)) +
  geom_bar(fill = "steelblue")+ theme_minimal()
```

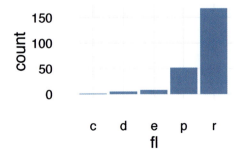

Part III

Plot Two Variables - X & Y: Both Continuous or Discrete

Chapter 12

Scatter plots: Continuous X and Y

12.1 Data format

We'll use the **mtcars** data set. The variable *cyl* is used as grouping variable.

```
data(mtcars)
mtcars$cyl <- as.factor(mtcars$cyl)
head(mtcars[, c("wt", "mpg", "cyl")], 3)
```

```
##                   wt  mpg cyl
## Mazda RX4      2.620 21.0   6
## Mazda RX4 Wag  2.875 21.0   6
## Datsun 710     2.320 22.8   4
```

12.2 Plot types

We start by creating a plot, named **b**, that we'll finish in the next section by adding a layer.

```
b <- ggplot(mtcars, aes(x = wt, y = mpg))
```

Possible layers include:

- **geom_point()** for scatter plot
- **geom_smooth()** for adding smoothed line such as regression line
- **geom_quantile()** for adding quantile lines
- **geom_rug()** for adding a marginal rug
- **geom_jitter()** for avoiding overplotting
- **geom_text()** for adding textual annotations

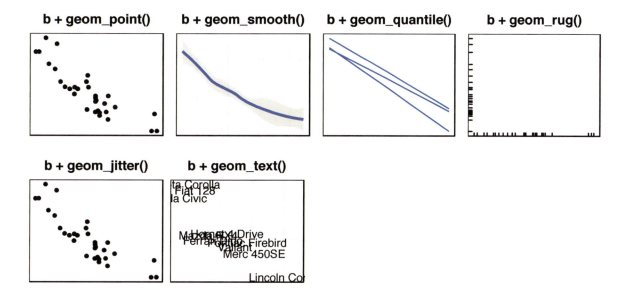

12.3   Basic scatter plots

The function **geom_point()** is used to create a **scatter plot**.

- **Key function**: *geom_point()*

- **Key arguments to customize the plot**: *alpha, color, fill, shape and size*

The color, the size and the shape of points can be changed using the function **geom_point()** as follow :

```
geom_point(size, color, shape)
```

> Note that, the size of the points can be also controlled by the values of a continuous variable.

```
# Basic scatter plot
b + geom_point(color = "#00AFBB")
```

```
# Change the point size, and shape
b + geom_point(color = "#00AFBB", size = 2, shape = 23)
```

```
# Control point size by continuous variable values
b + geom_point(aes(size=qsec), color = "#00AFBB")
```

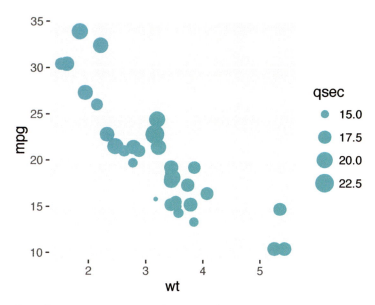

Read more on point shapes: Chapter 27

It's possible to use the function **geom_text**() for adding point labels:

```
b + geom_point() +
  geom_text(label=rownames(mtcars), nudge_x = 0.5)
```

Read more on text annotations : Chapter 34

12.4   Scatter plots with multiple groups

This section describes how to change point colors and shapes automatically and manually.

1. **Change the point color/shape/size automatically**: In the R code below, point shapes, colors and sizes are controlled automatically by the levels of the grouping variable *cyl* :

```
# Change point shapes by the levels of cyl
b + geom_point(aes(shape = cyl))

# Change point shapes and colors
b + geom_point(aes(shape = cyl, color = cyl))
```

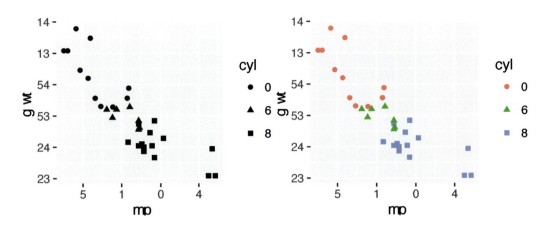

2. Change the point color/shape/size manually

The functions below are used :

- *scale_shape_manual()* for point shapes
- *scale_color_manual()* for point colors
- *scale_size_manual()* for point sizes

```
# Change the point sizes manually
b + geom_point(aes(color = cyl, shape = cyl, size = cyl)) +
  scale_size_manual(values=c(2,3,4))

# Change point shapes and colors manually
b + geom_point(aes(color = cyl, shape = cyl)) +
  scale_shape_manual(values=c(3, 16, 17))+
  scale_color_manual(values=c('#999999','#E69F00', '#56B4E9'))
```

- *scale_color_brewer()* : to use color palettes from *RColorBrewer* package
- *scale_color_grey()* : to use grey color palettes

```r
# use brewer color palettes
b + geom_point(aes(color = cyl, shape = cyl)) +
  scale_color_brewer(palette="Dark2") + theme_minimal()

# Use grey scale
b + geom_point(aes(color = cyl, shape = cyl)) +
  scale_color_grey()+ theme_minimal()
```

Read more on ggplot2 colors here : Chapter 26

12.5   Add regression line or smoothed conditional mean

- **Key functions**: *geom_smooth()* and *geom_abline()* (Chapter 35)
- **Alternative functions**: *stat_smooth()*
- **Key arguments to customize the plot**: *alpha, color, fill, shape, linetype and size*

Only the function **geom_smooth()** is covered in this section.

A simplified format is :

```
geom_smooth(method="auto", se=TRUE, fullrange=FALSE, level=0.95)
```

- **method** : smoothing method to be used. Possible values are lm, glm, gam, loess, rlm.
    - **method = "loess"**: This is the default value for small number of observations. It computes a smooth local regression. You can read more about **loess** using the R code **?loess**.
    - **method =“lm”**: It fits a **linear model**. Note that, it's also possible to indicate the formula as **formula = y ~ poly(x, 3)** to specify a degree 3 polynomial.
- **se** : logical value. If TRUE, confidence interval is displayed around smooth.
- **fullrange** : logical value. If TRUE, the fit spans the full range of the plot
- **level** : level of confidence interval to use. Default value is 0.95

To add a **regression line** on a scatter plot, the function **geom_smooth()** is used in combination with the argument **method = lm**. **lm** stands for **linear model**.

```
# Add regression line
b + geom_point() + geom_smooth(method = lm)

# Point + regression line
# Remove the confidence interval
b + geom_point() +
  geom_smooth(method = lm, se = FALSE)

# loess method: local regression fitting
b + geom_point() + geom_smooth()
```

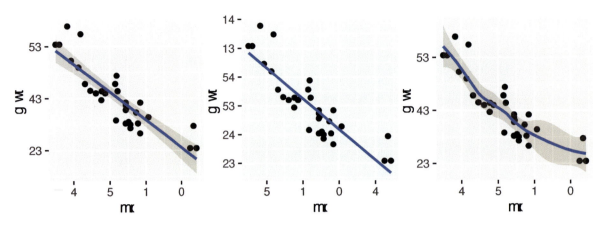

Change point color and shapes by groups:

```
# Change color and shape by groups (cyl)
b + geom_point(aes(color = cyl, shape=cyl)) +
  geom_smooth(aes(color = cyl, fill = cyl), method = lm)

# Remove confidence intervals
# Extend the regression lines: fullrange
b + geom_point(aes(color = cyl, shape = cyl)) +
  geom_smooth(aes(color = cyl), method = lm, se = FALSE,
              fullrange = TRUE)
```

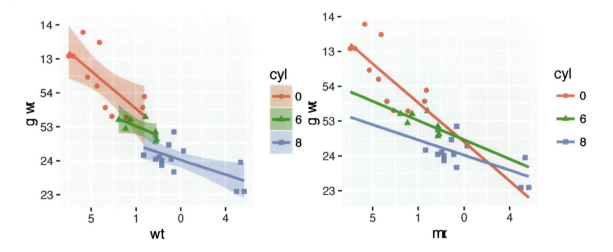

12.6 Add quantile lines from a quantile regression

Quantile lines can be used as a continuous analogue of a **geom_boxplot()**.

- **Key function**: *geom_quantile()*
- **Alternative functions**: *stat_quantile()*
- **Key arguments to customize the plot**: *alpha, color, linetype and size*

We'll use the **mpg** data set [in **ggplot2**].

The function **geom_quantile()** can be used for adding quantile lines:

```
ggplot(mpg, aes(cty, hwy)) +
  geom_point() + geom_quantile() +
  theme_minimal()
```

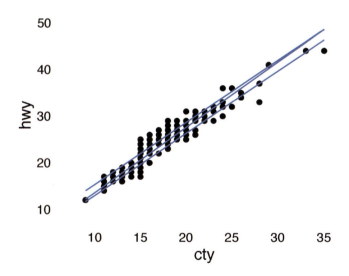

12.7   Add marginal rugs to a scatter plot

- **Key function**: *geom_rug()*

- **Key arguments to customize the plot**: *alpha, color and size*

The function **geom_rug()** can be used as follow :

```
geom_rug(sides ="bl")
```

Sides : a string that controls which sides of the plot the rugs appear on. Allowed value is a string containing any of "trbl", for top, right, bottom, and left.

```
# Add marginal rugs
b + geom_point() + geom_rug()

# Change colors by groups
b + geom_point(aes(color = cyl)) +
  geom_rug(aes(color = cyl))

# Add marginal rugs using faithful data
data(faithful)
ggplot(faithful, aes(x = eruptions, y = waiting)) +
  geom_point() + geom_rug()
```

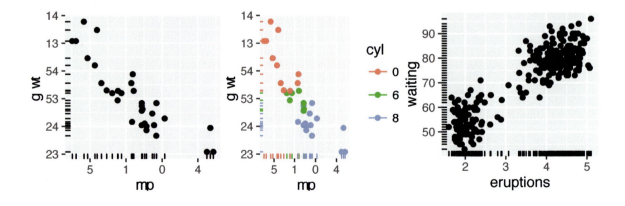

12.8   Jitter points to reduce overplotting

- **Key functions**: *geom_jitter()* and *position_jitter()*

- **Key arguments to customize the plot**: *alpha, color, fill, shape and size*

The function **geom_jitter()** is a convenient default for **geom_point(position = 'jitter')**. The **mpg** data set [in **ggplot2**] is used in the following examples.

```
p <- ggplot(mpg, aes(displ, hwy))
# Default scatter plot
p + geom_point()

# Use jitter to reduce overplotting
p + geom_jitter(position = position_jitter(width = 0.5, height = 0.5))
```

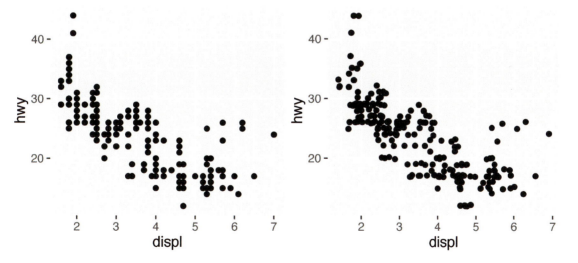

To adjust the extent of jittering, the function **position_jitter()** with the arguments **width** and **height** are used:

- **width**: degree of jitter in x direction.
- **height**: degree of jitter in y direction.

12.9   Textual annotations

> - **Key function**: *geom_text()*
>
> - **Key arguments to customize the plot**: *label, alpha, angle, color, family, fontface, hjust, lineheight, size, and vjust.*

The argument **label** is used to specify a vector of labels for point annotations.

```
b + geom_text(aes(label = rownames(mtcars)),
              size = 3)
```

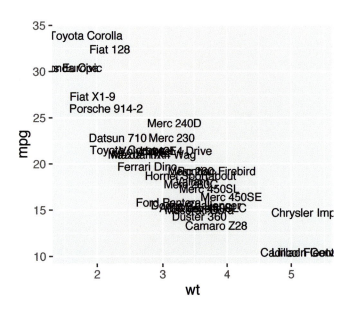

Chapter 13

Continuous bivariate distribution

13.1   Data format

We'll use the **diamonds** data set [in **ggplot2**]:

```
data(diamonds)
head(diamonds[, c("carat", "price")])
```

```
## Source: local data frame [6 x 2]
##
##    carat price
##    (dbl) (int)
## 1   0.23   326
## 2   0.21   326
## 3   0.23   327
## 4   0.29   334
## 5   0.31   335
## 6   0.24   336
```

13.2   Plot types

We start by creating a plot, named **c**, that we'll finish in the next section by adding a layer.

```r
c <- ggplot(diamonds, aes(carat, price))
```

Possible layers include:

- **geom_bin2d()** for adding a heatmap of **2d bin counts**. Rectangular bining.
- **geom_hex()** for adding **hexagon bining**. The R package **hexbin** is required for this functionality
- **geom_density_2d()** for adding contours from a **2d density** estimate

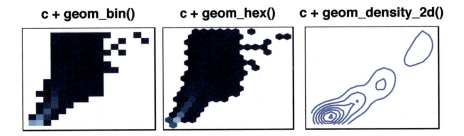

c + geom_bin()   **c + geom_hex()**   **c + geom_density_2d()**

13.3   Add heatmap of 2d bin counts

The function **geom_bin2d()** produces a scatter plot with rectangular bins. The number of observations is counted in each bins and displayed as a heatmap.

- **Key function:** *geom_bin2d()*

- **Alternative functions:** *stat_bin_2d(), stat_summary_2d()*

- **Key arguments to customize the plot:** *max, xmin, ymax, ymin, alpha, color, fill, linetype and size.*

```r
# Default plot
c + geom_bin2d()
```

```
# Change the number of bins
c + geom_bin2d(bins = 15)
```

```
# Or specify the width of bins
c + geom_bin2d(binwidth=c(1, 1000))
```

Alternative functions:

```
c + stat_bin_2d()
```

```
c + stat_summary_2d(aes(z = depth))
```

13.4   Add hexagon bining

The function **geom_hex()** produces a scatter plot with hexagon bining. The **hexbin** R package is required for hexagon bining. If you don't have it, use the R code below to install it:

```
install.packages("hexbin")
```

- **Key function**: *geom_hex()*

- **Alternative functions**: *stat_bin_hex(), stat_summary_hex()*

- **Key arguments to customize the plot**: *alpha, color, fill and size.*

The function **geom_hex()** can be used as follow:

```
require(hexbin)
# Default plot
c + geom_hex()

# Change the number of bins
c + geom_hex(bins = 10)
```

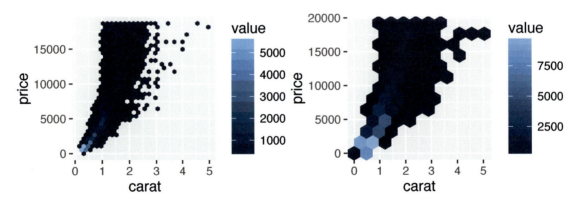

Alternative functions:

```
c + stat_bin_hex()
```

```
c + stat_summary_hex(aes(z = depth))
```

13.5 Scatter plots with 2d density estimation

The functions **geom_density_2d()** or **stat_density_2d()** can be used to add 2d density estimate to a scatter plot.

- **Key function**: *geom_density_2d()*

- **Alternative function**: *stat_density_2d()*

- **Key arguments to customize the plot**: *alpha, color, linetype and size.*

faithful data set is used in this section, and we first start by creating a scatter plot (*sp*) as follow:

```r
data("faithful")
# Scatter plot
sp <- ggplot(faithful, aes(x = eruptions, y = waiting))
```

```r
# Default plot
sp + geom_density_2d(color = "#E7B800")
# Add points
sp + geom_point(color = "#00AFBB") +
  geom_density_2d(color = "#E7B800")
```

```r
# Use stat_density_2d with geom = "polygon"
sp + geom_point() +
  stat_density_2d(aes(fill = ..level..), geom="polygon")

# Change the gradient color
sp + geom_point() +
  stat_density_2d(aes(fill = ..level..), geom="polygon") +
  scale_fill_gradient(low="#00AFBB", high="#FC4E07")
```

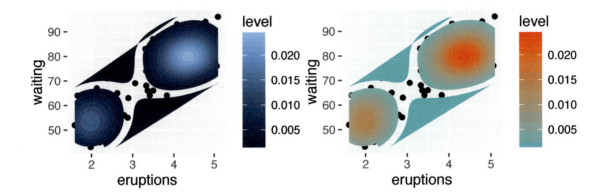

- Alternative function:

```r
sp + stat_density_2d()
```

- **See also**: *?stat_contour(), ?geom_contour()*

13.6   Continuous function

In this section, we'll see how to connect observations by **line**.

- **Key functions**: *geom_area(), geom_line(), geom_step()*

- **Key arguments to customize the plot**: *alpha, color, linetype, size and fill (for geom_area only).*

The **economics** data set [in **ggplot2**] is used.

```
data(economics)
# head(economics)
```

We start by creating a plot, named **d**, that we'll finish by adding a layer.

```
d <- ggplot(economics, aes(x = date, y = unemploy))
```

Possible layers include:

- **geom_area()** for area plot
- **geom_line()** for line plot connecting observations, ordered by x
- **geom_step()** for connecting observations by stairs

```
# Area plot
d + geom_area(fill = "#00AFBB", color = "white")

# Line plot: connecting observations, ordered by x
d + geom_line(color = "#E7B800")

# Connecting observations by stairs
# a subset of economics data set is used
set.seed(1234)
ss <- economics[sample(1:nrow(economics), 15), ]
ggplot(ss, aes(x = date, y = unemploy)) +
  geom_step(color = "#FC4E07")
```

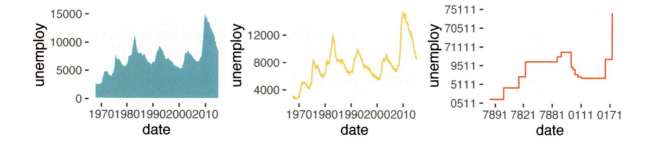

Chapter 14

Two variables: Discrete X, Discrete Y

- Key function: *geom_jitter()*
- Key arguments to customize the plot: *alpha, color, fill, shape and size.*

The **diamonds** data set [in **ggplot2**] we'll be used to plot the discrete variable **color** (for diamond colors) by the discrete variable **cut** (for diamond cut types). The plot is created using the function **geom_jitter()**.

```
data("diamonds")
ggplot(diamonds, aes(cut, color)) +
  geom_jitter(aes(color = cut), size = 0.5)
```

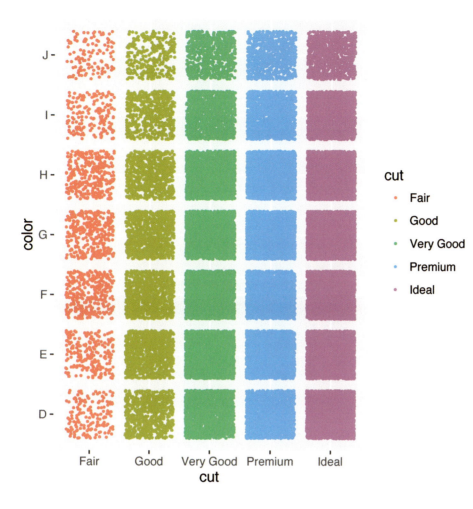

Part IV

Plot Two Variables - X & Y: Discrete X and Continuous Y

14.1 Data format

The **ToothGrowth** data set we'll be used to plot the continuous variable **len** (for tooth length) by the discrete variable **dose**. The following R code converts the variable **dose** from a numeric to a discrete factor variable.

```
data("ToothGrowth")
ToothGrowth$dose <- as.factor(ToothGrowth$dose)
head(ToothGrowth)
```

```
##     len supp dose
## 1   4.2   VC  0.5
## 2  11.5   VC  0.5
## 3   7.3   VC  0.5
## 4   5.8   VC  0.5
## 5   6.4   VC  0.5
## 6  10.0   VC  0.5
```

14.2 Plot types

We start by creating a plot, named **e**, that we'll finish in the next section by adding a layer.

```
e <- ggplot(ToothGrowth, aes(x = dose, y = len))
```

Possible layers include:

- **geom_boxplot()** for box plot
- **geom_violin()** for violin plot
- **geom_dotplot()** for dot plot
- **geom_jitter()** for stripchart
- **geom_line()** for line plot
- **geom_bar()** for bar plot

e + geom_boxplot()   **e + geom_violin()**   **e + geom_dotplot()**   **e + geom_jitter()**

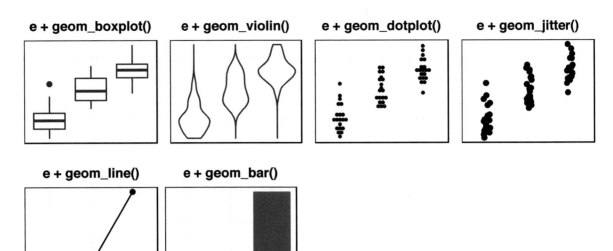

e + geom_line()   **e + geom_bar()**

Chapter 15

Box Plots

Box plots display a group of numerical data through their quartiles.

- **Key function**: *geom_boxplot()*

- **Alternative function**: *stat_boxplot()*

- **Key arguments to customize the plot**: *alpha, color, linetype, shape, size and fill.*

The function **geom_boxplot()** is used to create a **box plot**. A simplified format is :

```
geom_boxplot(outlier.colour = "black", outlier.shape = 16,
             outlier.size = 2, notch = FALSE)
```

- **outlier.colour**, **outlier.shape**, **outlier.size**: The color, the shape and the size for outlying points
- **notch**: logical value. If TRUE, makes a **notched box plot**. The notch displays a confidence interval around the median which is normally based on the median +/- 1.58*IQR/sqrt(n). Notches are used to compare groups; if the notches of two boxes do not overlap, this is a strong evidence that the medians differ.

15.1   Basic box plots

```
# Basic box plot
e + geom_boxplot()

# Rotate the box plot
e + geom_boxplot() + coord_flip()

# Notched box plot
e + geom_boxplot(notch = TRUE)

# Box plot with mean points
e + geom_boxplot() +
  stat_summary(fun.y = mean, geom = "point",
               shape = 18, size = 4, color = "blue")
```

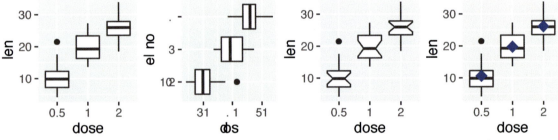

It's possible to use the function **scale__x__discrete()** for:

- choosing which items to display: for example c("0.5", "2"),

- changing the order of items: for example from c("0.5", "1", "2") to c("2", "0.5", "1")

```
# Choose which items to display: group "0.5" and "2"
e + geom_boxplot() +
  scale_x_discrete(limits=c("0.5", "2"))

# Change the default order of items
```

```
e + geom_boxplot() +
  scale_x_discrete(limits=c("2", "0.5", "1"))
```

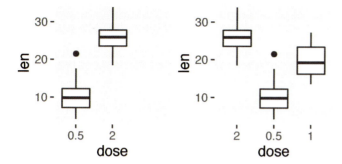

- **Alternative functions**: *stat_boxplot()*

```
e + stat_boxplot(coeff = 1.5)
```

15.2 Change colors by groups

Box plot outline and fill colors can be automatically controlled by the levels of the grouping variable *dose*:

```
# Use single colors
e + geom_boxplot(color = "black", fill = "steelblue")

# Change outline colors by dose (groups)
e + geom_boxplot(aes(color = dose))

# Change fill color by dose (groups)
e + geom_boxplot(aes(fill = dose))
```

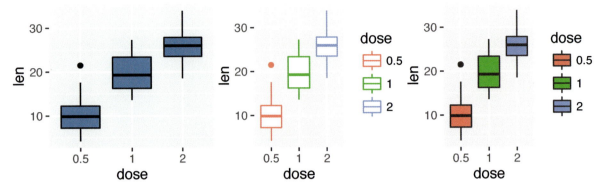

Change manually box plot outline/fill colors using the functions :

- *scale_color_manual(), scale_fill_manual()* : to use custom colors
- *scale_color_brewer(), scale_fill_brewer()* : to use color palettes from *RColor-Brewer* package
- *scale_color_grey(), scale_fill_grey()* : to use grey color palettes

Change manually outline colors:

```
# Use custom color palettes
e2 <- e + geom_boxplot(aes(color = dose)) + theme_minimal()
e2 + scale_color_manual(values=c("#999999", "#E69F00", "#56B4E9"))

# Use brewer color palettes
e2 + scale_color_brewer(palette="Dark2")

# Use grey scale
e2 + scale_color_grey()
```

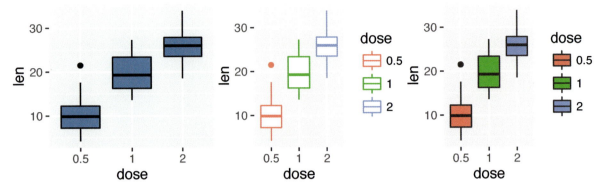

Change manually fill colors:

```r
# Use custom color palettes
e3 <- e + geom_boxplot(aes(fill = dose)) + theme_minimal()
e3 + scale_fill_manual(values=c("#999999", "#E69F00", "#56B4E9"))

# Use brewer color palettes
e3 + scale_fill_brewer(palette="Dark2")

# Use grey scale
e3 + scale_fill_grey()
```

Read more on ggplot2 colors here: Chapter 26

15.3 Box plot with multiple groups

The grouping variables **dose** and **supp** are used:

```r
# Change box plot colors by groups
e + geom_boxplot(aes(fill = supp))

# Change the position
e + geom_boxplot(aes(fill = supp), position = position_dodge(1))

# Change fill colors
e + geom_boxplot(aes(fill = supp), position = position_dodge(1)) +
  scale_fill_manual(values=c("#999999", "#E69F00"))
```

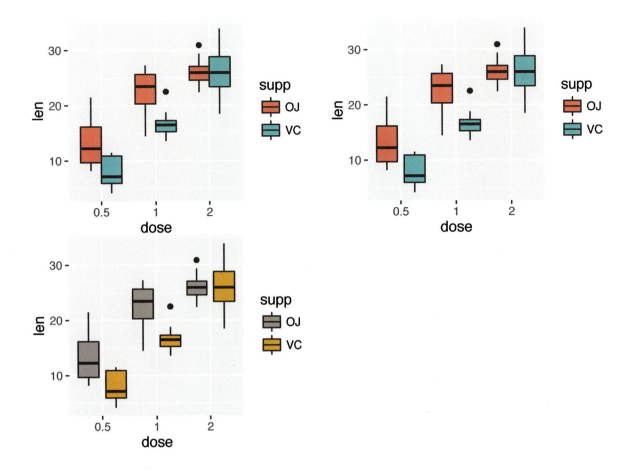

Chapter 16

Violin plots

Violin plots are similar to **box plots** (Chapter 15), except that they also show the kernel probability density of the data at different values. Typically, violin plots will include a marker for the median of the data and a box indicating the interquartile range, as in standard box plots.

The function **geom_violin()** is used to produce a violin plot.

- **Key function**: *geom_violin()*

- **Alternative function**: *stat_ydensity()*

- **Key arguments to customize the plot**: *alpha, color, linetype, size and fill.*

16.1 Basic violin plots

```
# Basic box plot
e + geom_violin()
# Rotate the violin plot
e + geom_violin() + coord_flip()
# Set trim argument to FALSE
e + geom_violin(trim = FALSE, fill = "steelblue")
```

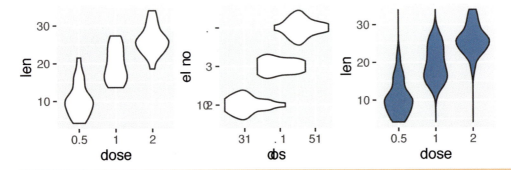

Note that by default *trim = TRUE*. In this case, the tails of the violins are trimmed. If *FALSE*, the tails are not trimmed.

To change the order of items (or to select some of the items), the function **scale_x_discrete()** can be used as described in Chapter 15.

16.2   Add summary statistics

The function **stat_summary()** can be used to add mean/median points and more on a violin plot

```
# Add mean or median point: use fun.y = mean or fun.y = median
e + geom_violin(trim = FALSE) +
    stat_summary(fun.y = mean, geom = "point",
                 shape = 23, size = 2, color = "blue")


# Add mean points +/- SD
# Use geom = "pointrange" or geom = "crossbar"
e + geom_violin(trim = FALSE) +
  stat_summary(fun.data="mean_sdl",  fun.args = list(mult=1),
               geom="pointrange", color = "red")


# Combine with box plot to add median and quartiles
e + geom_violin(trim = FALSE) +
    geom_boxplot(width = 0.2)
```

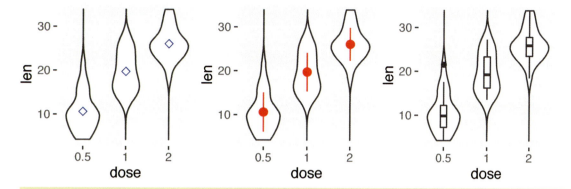

The function *mean_sdl* is used for adding mean and standard deviation. It computes the *mean* plus or minus a *constant* times the *standard deviation*. In the R code above, the constant is specified using the argument *mult* (mult = 1). By default mult = 2. The mean +/- SD can be added as a *crossbar* or a *pointrange*.

16.3   Change colors by groups

Violin plot outline and fill colors can be automatically controlled by the levels of the grouping variable *dose*:

```r
# Change outline colors by dose (groups)
e + geom_violin(aes(color = dose), trim = FALSE)

# Change fill color by dose (groups)
e + geom_violin(aes(fill = dose), trim = FALSE)
```

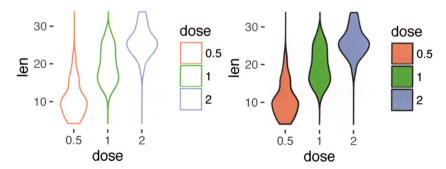

As described in box plot chapter (Chapter 15), it's possible to change manually violin plot outline/fill colors, as follow:

```r
# Change manually outline colors
e2 <- e + geom_violin(aes(color = dose), trim = FALSE) + theme_minimal()
e2 + scale_color_manual(values=c("#999999", "#E69F00", "#56B4E9"))

# Change manually fill colors
e3 <- e + geom_violin(aes(fill = dose), trim = FALSE) + theme_minimal()
e3 + scale_fill_manual(values=c("#999999", "#E69F00", "#56B4E9"))
```

Read more on ggplot2 colors here: Chapter 26

16.4   Violin plots with multiple groups

The grouping variables **dose** and **supp** are used:

```r
# Change colors by groups
e + geom_violin(aes(fill = supp), trim = FALSE)

# Change fill colors
e + geom_violin(aes(fill = supp), trim = FALSE) +
  scale_fill_manual(values=c("#999999", "#E69F00"))
```

Chapter 17

Dot Plots

The function **geom_dotplot()** is used to create a **dot plot**.

> - **Key functions**: *geom_dotplot(), stat_summary()*
>
> - **Key arguments to customize the plot**: *alpha, color, dotsize and fill.*

17.1   Basic dot plots

```
# Basic plot
e + geom_dotplot(binaxis = "y", stackdir = "center")

# Change dotsize and stack ratio
e + geom_dotplot(binaxis = "y", stackdir = "center",
                 stackratio = 1.5, dotsize = 1.1)
```

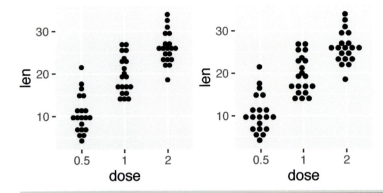

> To change the order of items (or to select some of the items), the function **scale_x_discrete()** can be used as described in Chapter 15

17.2   Add summary statistics

The function **stat_summary()** can be used to add mean/median points and more on a violin plot

```
# Add mean or median point: use fun.y = mean or fun.y = median
e + geom_dotplot(binaxis = "y", stackdir = "center") +
    stat_summary(fun.y = mean, geom = "point",
                 shape = 18, size = 3, color = "red")

# Add mean points +/- SD
# Use geom = "pointrange" or geom = "crossbar"
e + geom_dotplot(binaxis = "y", stackdir = "center") +
  stat_summary(fun.data="mean_sdl",  fun.args = list(mult=1),
               geom="pointrange", color = "red")
```

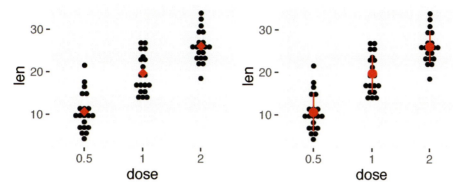

Combine with box plot and dot plot:

```
# Combine with box plot
e + geom_boxplot() +
  geom_dotplot(binaxis = "y", stackdir = "center")
```

```
# Combine with violin plot
e + geom_violin(trim = FALSE) +
  geom_dotplot(binaxis='y', stackdir='center')
```

```
# Dot plot + violin plot + stat summary
e + geom_violin(trim = FALSE) +
  geom_dotplot(binaxis='y', stackdir='center') +
  stat_summary(fun.data="mean_sdl",  fun.args = list(mult=1),
               geom="pointrange", color = "red")
```

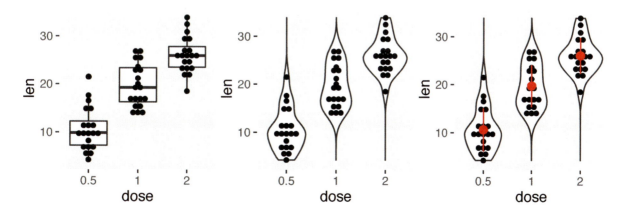

17.3   Change colors by groups

Dot plot outline and fill colors can be automatically controlled by the levels of the grouping variable *dose*:

```
# Use single colors
e + geom_dotplot(binaxis='y', stackdir='center', color = "black",
                 fill = "lightgray") + theme_minimal()

# Change outline colors by dose (groups)
e + geom_dotplot(aes(color = dose), binaxis='y', stackdir='center',
                 fill = "white") + theme_minimal()

# Change fill color by dose (groups)
e + geom_dotplot(aes(fill = dose), binaxis='y', stackdir='center') +
    theme_minimal()
```

As described in box plot chapter (Chapter 15), it's possible to change manually dot plot outline/fill colors, as follow:

```
# Change manually outline colors
# Use custom color palettes
e2 <- e + geom_dotplot(aes(color = dose), binaxis='y',
               stackdir='center', fill = "white") + theme_minimal()
e2 + scale_color_manual(values=c("#999999", "#E69F00", "#56B4E9"))

# Change manually fill colors
# Use custom color palettes
```

```
e3 <- e + geom_dotplot(aes(fill = dose), binaxis='y',
                    stackdir='center') + theme_minimal()
e3 + scale_fill_manual(values=c("#999999", "#E69F00", "#56B4E9"))
```

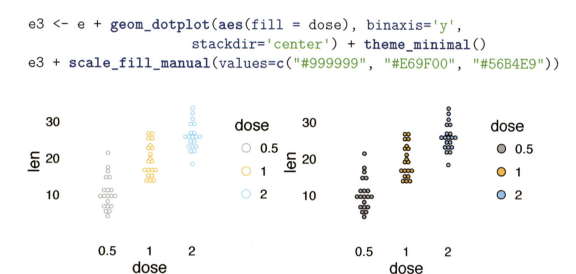

Read more on ggplot2 colors here: Chapter 26

17.4   Dot plot with multiple groups

The grouping variables **dose** and **supp** are used:

```
# Change colors by groups
e + geom_dotplot(aes(fill = supp), binaxis='y', stackdir='center')

# Change the position : interval between dot plot of the same group
e + geom_dotplot(aes(fill = supp), binaxis='y', stackdir='center',
                position=position_dodge(0.8))
```

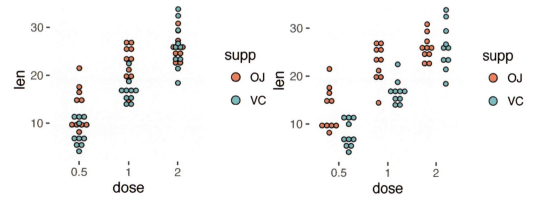

Change dot plot colors and add box plots :

```
# Change colors
e + geom_dotplot(aes(fill = supp), binaxis='y', stackdir='center',
                 position=position_dodge(0.8)) +
  scale_fill_manual(values=c("#999999", "#E69F00"))

# Add box plots
e + geom_boxplot(fill = "white") +
  geom_dotplot(aes(fill = supp), binaxis='y', stackdir='center')

# Change the position
e + geom_boxplot(aes(fill = supp), position=position_dodge(0.8))+
    geom_dotplot(aes(fill = supp), binaxis='y', stackdir='center',
                 position=position_dodge(0.8))
```

Chapter 18

Stripcharts

Stripcharts are also known as one dimensional scatter plots. These plots are suitable compared to box plots when sample sizes are small.

The function **geom_jitter()** is used.

- **Key functions**: *geom_jitter(), stat_summary()*

- **Key arguments to customize the plot**: *alpha, color, shape, size and fill.*

18.1   Basic stripcharts

```
# Basic plot
e + geom_jitter()

# Change the position
# 0.2 : degree of jitter in x direction
e + geom_jitter(position = position_jitter(0.2))

# Change point shapes and size
e + geom_jitter(position=position_jitter(0.2),
           shape=17, size = 1.2)
```

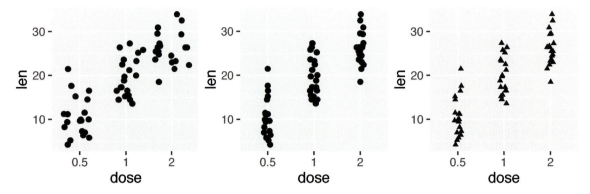

Read more on point shapes: Chapter 27.

18.2   Add summary statistics

The function **stat_summary**() can be used to add mean/median points and more
on a violin plot

```
# Add mean or median point: use fun.y = mean or fun.y = median
e + geom_jitter(position = position_jitter(0.2)) +
    stat_summary(fun.y = mean, geom = "point",
                 shape = 18, size = 3, color = "red")

# Add mean points +/- SD
# Use geom = "pointrange" or geom = "crossbar"
e + geom_jitter(position = position_jitter(0.2))+
   stat_summary(fun.data="mean_sdl",  fun.args = list(mult=1),
                geom="pointrange", color = "red")
```

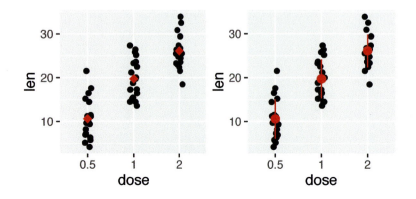

Combine with box plot and violin plot:

```
# Combine with box plot
e + geom_boxplot() +
  geom_jitter(position = position_jitter(0.2))


# Combine with violin plot
e + geom_violin(trim = FALSE) +
  geom_jitter(position = position_jitter(0.2))

# Strip chart + violin plot + stat summary
e + geom_violin(trim = FALSE) +
  geom_jitter(position = position_jitter(0.2)) +
  stat_summary(fun.data="mean_sdl",  fun.args = list(mult=1),
               geom="pointrange", color = "red")
```

18.3   Change point shapes by groups

In the R code below, point shapes are controlled automatically by the variable *dose*.
You can also set point shapes manually using the function **scale_shape_manual()**

```
# Change point shapes by groups
e + geom_jitter(aes(shape = dose), position=position_jitter(0.2))

# Change point shapes manually
```

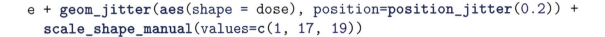

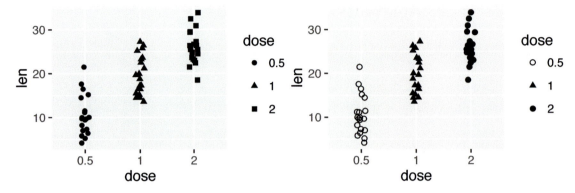

Read more on point shapes : Chapter 27

18.4 Change colors by groups

Point colors can be automatically controlled by the levels of the grouping variable *dose*:

```
# Use single colors
e + geom_jitter(position = position_jitter(0.2), color = "steelblue") +
  theme_minimal()
```

```
# Change point colors by dose (groups)
e + geom_jitter(aes(color = dose), position = position_jitter(0.2)) +
  theme_minimal()
```

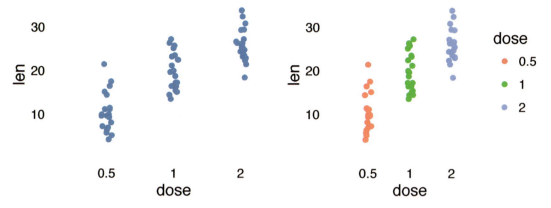

Change manually point colors using the functions :

- *scale_color_manual()*: to use custom colors
- *scale_color_brewer()*: to use color palettes from *RColorBrewer* package
- *scale_color_grey()*: to use grey color palettes

Change manually point colors:

```r
# Use custom color palettes
e3 <- e + geom_jitter(aes(color = dose), position = position_jitter(0.2)) +
        theme_minimal()
e3 + scale_fill_manual(values=c("#999999", "#E69F00", "#56B4E9"))

# Use brewer color palettes
e3 + scale_color_brewer(palette="Dark2")
```

Read more on ggplot2 colors here: Chapter 26

18.5   Stripchart with multiple groups

The grouping variables **dose** and **supp** are used:

```
# Change colors and shapes by groups
e + geom_jitter(aes(color = supp, shape = supp),
                position=position_jitter(0.2))


# Change the position : interval between dot plot of the same group
e + geom_jitter(aes(color = supp, shape = supp),
                position=position_dodge(0.2))
```

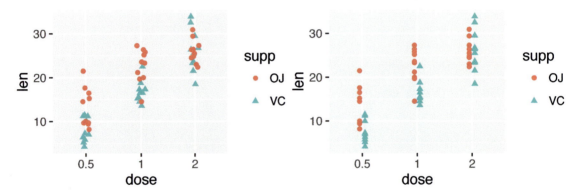

Change point plot colors and add box plots :

```
# Change colors
e + geom_jitter(aes(color = supp, shape = supp),
                position=position_jitter(0.2))+
  scale_color_manual(values=c("#999999", "#E69F00"))


# Add box plots
e + geom_boxplot(color = "black") +
  geom_jitter(aes(color = supp, shape = supp),
              position=position_jitter(0.2))


# Change the position
e + geom_boxplot(aes(color = supp), position=position_dodge(0.8)) +
  geom_jitter(aes(color = supp, shape = supp),
              position=position_dodge(0.8))
```

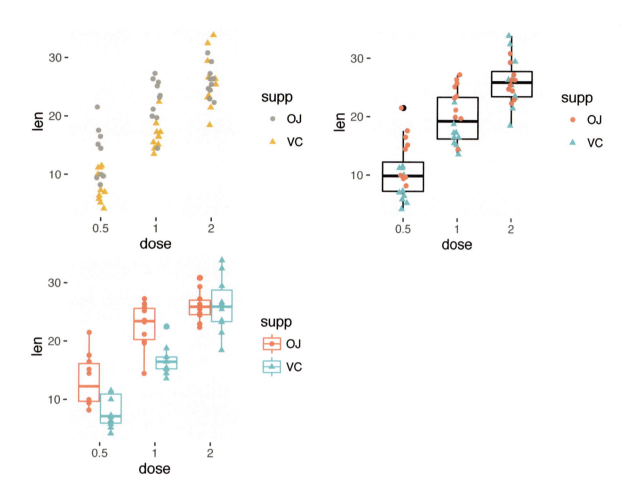

Chapter 19

Line Plots

In a line graph, observations are ordered by x value and connected.

x value (for x axis) can be :

- date : for a time series data
- texts
- discrete numeric values
- continuous numeric values

The functions **geom_line()**, **geom_step()** or **geom_path()** can be used to generate line plots.

- **Key functions:** *geom_line(), geom_step(), geom_path()*

- **Key arguments to customize the plot:** *alpha, color, linetype and size.*

19.1 Data format

Data derived from *ToothGrowth* data sets are used.

```r
df <- data.frame(dose=c("D0.5", "D1", "D2"),
                 len=c(4.2, 10, 29.5))

head(df)
```

```
##   dose  len
## 1 D0.5  4.2
## 2   D1 10.0
## 3   D2 29.5
```

```r
df2 <- data.frame(supp=rep(c("VC", "OJ"), each=3),
                  dose=rep(c("D0.5", "D1", "D2"),2),
                  len=c(6.8, 15, 33, 4.2, 10, 29.5))

head(df2)
```

```
##   supp dose  len
## 1   VC D0.5  6.8
## 2   VC   D1 15.0
## 3   VC   D2 33.0
## 4   OJ D0.5  4.2
## 5   OJ   D1 10.0
## 6   OJ   D2 29.5
```

- *len* : Tooth length
- *dose* : Dose in milligrams (0.5, 1, 2)
- *supp* : Supplement type (VC or OJ)

19.2   Basic line plots

```r
p <- ggplot(data=df, aes(x=dose, y=len, group=1))
# Basic line plot with points
p + geom_line() + geom_point()
```

```
# Change line type and color
p + geom_line(linetype = "dashed", color = "steelblue")+
  geom_point(color = "steelblue")
```

```
# Use geom_step()
p + geom_step() + geom_point()
```

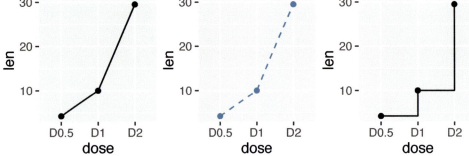

Read more on line types : Chapter 28

- **geom_line()** : Connect observations, ordered by x value
- **geom_path()** : Observations are connected in original order
- **geom_step()** : Connect observations by stairs

19.3   Line plot with multiple groups

In the graphs below, line types and point shapes are controlled automatically by the levels of the variable *supp* :

```
p <- ggplot(df2, aes(x=dose, y=len, group=supp))
# Change line types and point shapes by groups
p + geom_line(aes(linetype = supp)) +
   geom_point(aes(shape = supp))
```

```
# Change line types, point shapes and colors
p + geom_line(aes(linetype=supp, color = supp))+
   geom_point(aes(shape=supp, color = supp))
```

```
# Change color manually: custom color
p + geom_line(aes(linetype=supp, color = supp))+
    geom_point(aes(shape=supp, color = supp)) +
    scale_color_manual(values=c("#999999", "#E69F00"))
```

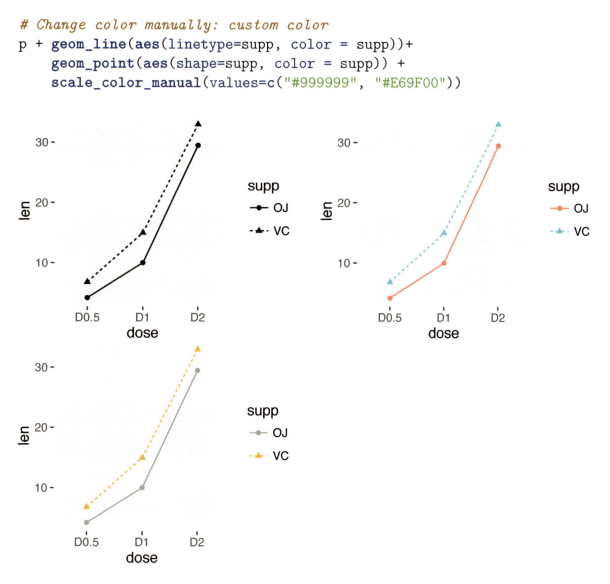

- Read more on line types: Chapter 28
- Read more on point shapes: Chapter 27
- Read more on ggplot2 colors: Chapter 26

19.4 Line plot with a numeric x-axis

If the variable on x-axis is numeric, it can be useful to treat it as a continuous or a factor variable depending on what you want to do:

```r
# Create some data
df3 <- data.frame(supp=rep(c("VC", "OJ"), each=3),
                  dose=rep(c("0.5", "1", "2"),2),
                  len=c(6.8, 15, 33, 4.2, 10, 29.5))
head(df3)
```

```
##    supp dose  len
## 1    VC  0.5  6.8
## 2    VC    1 15.0
## 3    VC    2 33.0
## 4    OJ  0.5  4.2
## 5    OJ    1 10.0
## 6    OJ    2 29.5
```

```r
# x axis treated as continuous variable
df3$dose <- as.numeric(as.vector(df3$dose))
ggplot(data=df3, aes(x = dose, y = len, group = supp, color = supp)) +
  geom_line() + geom_point()

# Axis treated as discrete variable
df2$dose<-as.factor(df3$dose)
ggplot(data=df2, aes(x = dose, y = len, group = supp, color = supp)) +
  geom_line() + geom_point()
```

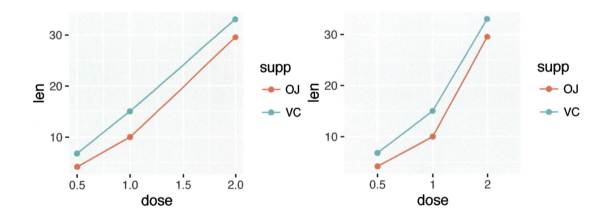

19.5 Line plot with dates on x-axis: Time series

economics time series data sets are used :

```
head(economics)
```

```
## Source: local data frame [6 x 6]
##
##           date    pce     pop psavert uempmed unemploy
##         (date)  (dbl)   (int)   (dbl)   (dbl)    (int)
## 1 1967-07-01  507.4  198712    12.5     4.5     2944
## 2 1967-08-01  510.5  198911    12.5     4.7     2945
## 3 1967-09-01  516.3  199113    11.7     4.6     2958
## 4 1967-10-01  512.9  199311    12.5     4.9     3143
## 5 1967-11-01  518.1  199498    12.5     4.7     3066
## 6 1967-12-01  525.8  199657    12.1     4.8     3018
```

Plots :

```
# Basic line plot
ggplot(data=economics, aes(x = date, y = pop))+
  geom_line()

# Plot a subset of the data
ss <- subset(economics, date > as.Date("2006-1-1"))
ggplot(data = ss, aes(x = date, y = pop)) + geom_line()
```

Change line size :

```
# Change line size
ggplot(data = economics, aes(x = date, y = pop, size = unemploy/pop)) +
  geom_line()
```

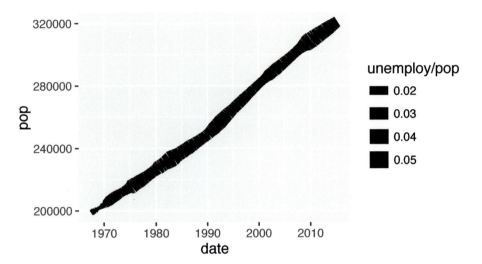

Plot multiple time series data:

```
# Solution 1
ggplot(economics, aes(x=date)) +
  geom_line(aes(y = psavert), color = "darkred") +
  geom_line(aes(y = uempmed), color="steelblue", linetype="twodash") +
  theme_minimal()
```

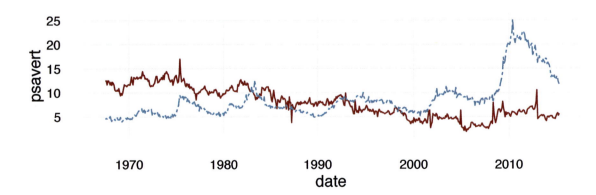

```
# Solution 2: melt by date.
require(reshape2)
df <- melt(economics[, c("date", "psavert", "uempmed")], id="date")
ggplot(df, aes(x = date, y = value)) +
  geom_line(aes(color = variable), size=1) +
  scale_color_manual(values = c("#999999", "#E69F00")) +
  theme_minimal()
```

```
# Area plot
ggplot(economics, aes(x=date)) +
  geom_area(aes(y=psavert), fill = "#999999",
            color = "#999999", alpha=0.5) +
  geom_area(aes(y=uempmed), fill = "#E69F00",
            color = "#E69F00",  alpha=0.5) +
  theme_minimal()
```

Chapter 20

Bar Plots

The function **geom_bar()** can be used to create a **bar plot**.

> - **Key function**: *geom_bar()*
> - **Key arguments to customize the plot**: *alpha, color, fill, linetype and size.*

20.1   Data format

We'll use the same data sets **df** and **df2** described in Chapter 19.

Data derived from *ToothGrowth* data sets are used.

```
df <- data.frame(dose=c("D0.5", "D1", "D2"),
                len=c(4.2, 10, 29.5))

# head(df)

df2 <- data.frame(supp=rep(c("VC", "OJ"), each=3),
                dose=rep(c("D0.5", "D1", "D2"),2),
                len=c(6.8, 15, 33, 4.2, 10, 29.5))

# head(df2)
```

20.2 Basic bar plots

We start by creating a simple **bar plot** (named **f**) using the *df* data set:

```
f <- ggplot(df, aes(x = dose, y = len))
```

```
# Basic bar plot
f + geom_bar(stat = "identity")
```

```
# Change fill color and add labels at the top (vjust = -0.3)
f + geom_bar(stat = "identity", fill = "steelblue")+
  geom_text(aes(label = len), vjust = -0.3, size = 3.5)+
  theme_minimal()
```

```
# Label inside bars, vjust = 1.6
f + geom_bar(stat="identity", fill="steelblue")+
  geom_text(aes(label=len), vjust=1.6, color="white", size=3.5)+
  theme_minimal()
```

It's possible to change the width of bars using the argument **width** (e.g.: width = 0.5)

To change the order of items (or to select some of the items), the function **scale_x_discrete()** can be used as described in Chapter 15

20.3   Change color by groups

```
# Change bar plot line colors by groups
f + geom_bar(aes(color = dose), stat="identity", fill="white")

# Change bar plot fill colors by groups
f + geom_bar(aes(fill = dose), stat="identity")

# Change outline color manually: custom color
f + geom_bar(aes(color = dose), stat="identity", fill="white") +
  scale_color_manual(values = c("#999999", "#E69F00", "#56B4E9"))

# Change fill color manually: custom color
f + geom_bar(aes(fill = dose), stat="identity") +
  scale_fill_manual(values = c("#999999", "#E69F00", "#56B4E9"))
```

20.4 Bar plot with multiple groups

```
g <- ggplot(data=df2, aes(x=dose, y=len, fill=supp))

# Stacked bar plot
g + geom_bar(stat = "identity")

# Use position=position_dodge()
g + geom_bar(stat="identity", position=position_dodge())
```

Add labels to a dodged bar plot :

```
ggplot(data=df2, aes(x=dose, y=len, fill=supp)) +
  geom_bar(stat="identity", position = position_dodge())+
  geom_text(aes(label = len), vjust = 1.6, color = "white",
            position = position_dodge(0.9), size = 3.5)
```

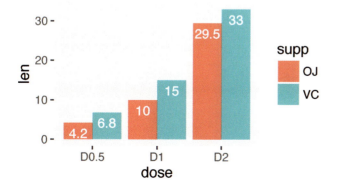

Add labels to a stacked bar plot: 3 steps are required

1. Sort the data by dose and supp : the package **plyr** is used
2. Calculate the cumulative sum of the variable *len* for each dose
3. Create the plot

```r
require(plyr)
# Sort by dose and supp
df_sorted <- arrange(df2, dose, supp)
head(df_sorted)
```

```
##    supp dose  len
## 1    OJ D0.5  4.2
## 2    VC D0.5  6.8
## 3    OJ   D1 10.0
## 4    VC   D1 15.0
## 5    OJ   D2 29.5
## 6    VC   D2 33.0
```

```r
# Calculate the cumulative sum of len for each dose
df_cumsum <- ddply(df_sorted, "dose", transform,
                   label_ypos=cumsum(len))
head(df_cumsum)
```

```
##    supp dose  len label_ypos
## 1    OJ D0.5  4.2        4.2
## 2    VC D0.5  6.8       11.0
## 3    OJ   D1 10.0       10.0
## 4    VC   D1 15.0       25.0
## 5    OJ   D2 29.5       29.5
## 6    VC   D2 33.0       62.5
```

```r
# Create the bar plot
ggplot(data=df_cumsum, aes(x = dose, y = len, fill = supp)) +
  geom_bar(stat = "identity")+
  geom_text(aes(y = label_ypos, label = len), vjust=1.6,
            color = "white", size = 3.5)
```

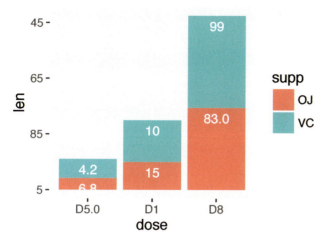

If you want to place the labels at the middle of bars, you have to modify the cumulative sum as follow :

```
df_cumsum <- ddply(df_sorted, "dose", transform,
                   label_ypos = cumsum(len) - 0.5*len)

# Create the bar plot
ggplot(data=df_cumsum, aes(x = dose, y = len, fill = supp)) +
  geom_bar(stat = "identity")+
  geom_text(aes(y = label_ypos, label = len), vjust = 1.6,
            color = "white", size = 3.5)
```

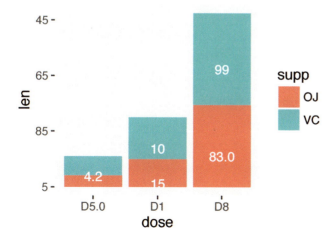

Chapter 21

Visualizing Error

21.1 Data format

The **ToothGrowth** data set we'll be used. We start by creating a data set named **df** which holds **ToothGrowth** data.

```
# ToothGrowth data set
df <- ToothGrowth
df$dose <- as.factor(df$dose)
head(df, 3)
```

```
##    len supp dose
## 1  4.2   VC  0.5
## 2 11.5   VC  0.5
## 3  7.3   VC  0.5
```

21.2 Compute mean and standard deviation

Using dplyr package, the following R code creates a data set named **df2** which holds the mean and the SD of tooth length (*len*) by groups (*dose*).

```r
library("dplyr")
df2 <- df %>%
  group_by(dose) %>%
  summarise(
    sd = sd(len),
    len = mean(len)
  )

head(df2)
```

```
## Source: local data frame [3 x 3]
##
##     dose       sd      len
##   (fctr)    (dbl)    (dbl)
## 1    0.5 4.499763   10.605
## 2      1 4.415436   19.735
## 3      2 3.774150   26.100
```

21.3   Plot types

We start by creating a plot, named **f**, that we'll finish in the next section by adding a layer.

```r
f <- ggplot(df2, aes(x = dose, y = len,
                 ymin = len-sd, ymax = len+sd))
```

Possible layers include:

- **geom_crossbar()** for hollow bar with middle indicated by horizontal line
- **geom_errorbar()** for error bars
- **geom_errorbarh()** for horizontal error bars
- **geom_linerange()** for drawing an interval represented by a vertical line
- **geom_pointrange()** for creating an interval represented by a vertical line, with a point in the middle.

f + geom_crossbar()   f + geom_errorbar()   f + geom_linerange()   f + geom_pointrange()

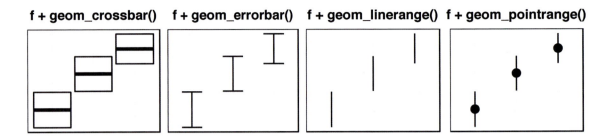

21.4   Cross bar

Cross bar is a hollow bar with middle indicated by horizontal line.

- **Key function**: *geom_crossbar(), stat_summary()*
- **Key arguments to customize the plot**: *alpha, color, fill, linetype and size.*

We'll use the data set named **df2**, which holds the mean and the SD of tooth length (*len*) by groups (*dose*).

```
# Default plot
f + geom_crossbar()

# color by groups
f + geom_crossbar(aes(color = dose))

# Change color manually
f + geom_crossbar(aes(color = dose)) +
  scale_color_manual(values = c("#999999", "#E69F00", "#56B4E9"))+
  theme_minimal()

# fill by groups and change color manually
f + geom_crossbar(aes(fill = dose)) +
  scale_fill_manual(values = c("#999999", "#E69F00", "#56B4E9"))+
  theme_minimal()
```

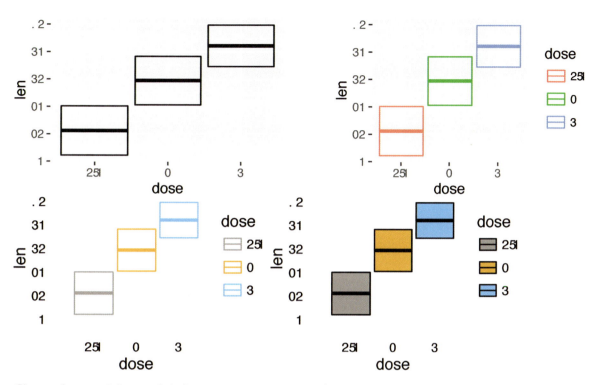

Cross bar with multiple groups: we start by creating a data set named **df3** which holds the mean and the SD of tooth length (*len*) by 2 groups (*supp* and *dose*).

```
library("dplyr")
df3 <- df %>%
  group_by(supp, dose) %>%
  summarise(
    sd = sd(len),
    len = mean(len)
  )
head(df3)
```

```
## Source: local data frame [3 x 4]
## Groups: supp [1]
##
##    supp   dose     sd    len
##   (fctr) (fctr)   (dbl)  (dbl)
## 1    OJ    0.5 4.459709  13.23
## 2    OJ      1 3.910953  22.70
## 3    OJ      2 2.655058  26.06
```

The data set **df3** is used to create **cross bars with multiple groups**. For this end, the variable **len** is plotted by **dose** and the color is changed by the levels of the factor **supp**.

```
f <- ggplot(df3, aes(x = dose, y = len,
                     ymin = len-sd, ymax = len+sd))
# Default plot
f + geom_crossbar(aes(color = supp))

# Use position_dodge() to avoid overlap
f + geom_crossbar(aes(color = supp),
                  position = position_dodge(1))
```

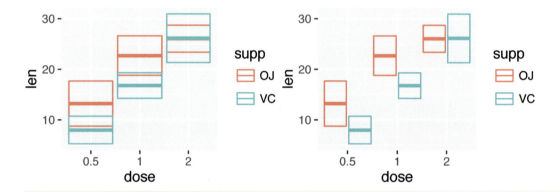

```
f <- ggplot(df, aes(x = dose, y = len, color = supp))
# Use geom_crossbar()
f + stat_summary(fun.data="mean_sdl", fun.args = list(mult=1),
                 geom="crossbar", width = 0.6,
                 position = position_dodge(0.8))
```

21.5 Error bar

> - **Key functions**: *geom_errorbar(), stat_summary()*
>
> - **Key arguments to customize the plot**: *alpha, color, linetype, size and width.*

We'll use the data set named **df2**, which holds the mean and the SD of tooth length (*len*) by groups (*dose*).

We start by creating a plot, named **f**, that we'll finish next by adding a layer.

```
f <- ggplot(df2, aes(x = dose, y = len,
                     ymin = len-sd, ymax = len+sd))
```

```
# Error bars colored by groups
f + geom_errorbar(aes(color = dose), width = 0.2)

# Combine with line plot
f + geom_line(aes(group = 1)) +
  geom_errorbar(width = 0.2)

# Combine with bar plot, color by groups
f + geom_bar(aes(color = dose), stat = "identity", fill ="white") +
  geom_errorbar(aes(color = dose), width = 0.2)

# Keep only upper error bars
f + geom_bar(aes(color = dose), stat="identity", fill ="white") +
  geom_errorbar(aes(color = dose, ymin = len), width=.2)
```

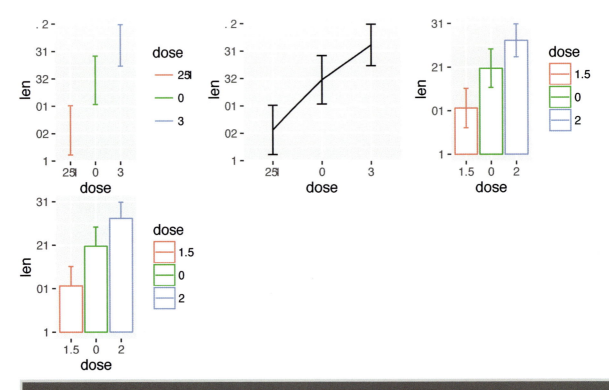

In the R code above, the argument **width** specifies the width of error bars.

Error bars with multiple groups:

The data set **df3** is used to create **cross bars with multiple groups**. For this end, the variable **len** is plotted by **dose** and the color is changed by the levels of the factor **supp**.

```
f <- ggplot(df3, aes(x = dose, y = len,
                     ymin = len-sd, ymax = len+sd))
# Bar plot with error bar
f + geom_bar(aes(fill = supp), stat = "identity",
             position = "dodge") +
  geom_errorbar(aes(color = supp),  position = "dodge")

# Line plot with error bar
f + geom_line(aes(group = supp, color = supp)) +
    geom_point(aes(color = supp))+
    geom_errorbar(aes(color = supp), width=.2,
                  position = position_dodge(0.05))
```

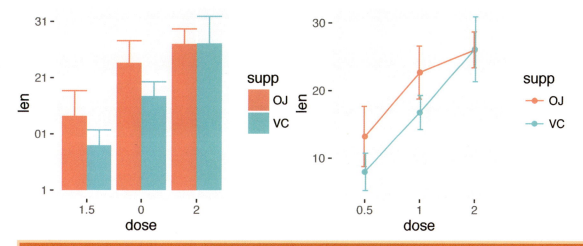

You can also use the functions **geom_pointrange()** or **geom_linerange()** instead of using **geom_errorbar()**

21.6   Horizontal error bar

- **Key function**: *geom_errorbarh()*

- **Key arguments to customize the plot**: *alpha, color, linetype, size and height.*

We'll use the data set named **df2**, which holds the mean and the SD of tooth length (*len*) by groups (*dose*).

We start by creating a plot, named **f**, that we'll finish next by adding a layer.

The arguments **xmin** and **xmax** are used for horizontal error bars.

```
f <- ggplot(df2, aes(x = len, y = dose ,
                xmin = len-sd, xmax = len+sd))
```

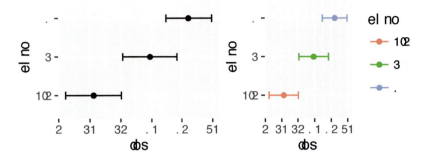

21.7   Interval represented by a vertical line

- **Key functions**: *geom_linerange(), geom_pointrange()*

- **Key arguments to customize the plot**: *alpha, color, linetype, size, shape and fill (for geom_pointrange()).*

- **geom_linerange()**: Add an interval represented by a vertical line
- **geom_pointrange()**: Add an interval represented by a vertical line with a point in the middle

We'll use the data set **df2**.

```
f <- ggplot(df2, aes(x = dose, y = len,
                     ymin=len-sd, ymax=len+sd))
# Line range
f + geom_linerange()

# Point range
f + geom_pointrange()
```

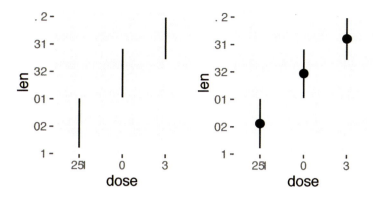

21.8   Combine dot plot and error bars

- **Key functions**: *geom_errorbarh(), geom_errorbar(), geom_linerange(), geom_pointrange(), geom_crossbar(), stat_summary()*

- **Key arguments to customize the plot**: *alpha, color, fill, linetype and size.*

To combine **geom_dotplot()** and **error bars**, we'll use the **ToothGrowth** data set. You don't need to compute the *mean* and *SD*. This can be done automatically by using the function **stat_summary()** in combination with the argument **fun.data = "mean_sdl"**.

We start by creating a dot plot, named **g**, that we'll finish in the next section by adding error bar layers.

```
g <- ggplot(df, aes(x=dose, y=len)) +
  geom_dotplot(binaxis='y', stackdir='center')
```

```
# use geom_crossbar()
g + stat_summary(fun.data="mean_sdl", fun.args = list(mult=1),
                 geom="crossbar", width=0.5)
```

```
# Use geom_errorbar()
```

```
g + stat_summary(fun.data=mean_sdl, fun.args = list(mult=1),
        geom="errorbar", color="red", width=0.2) +
  stat_summary(fun.y=mean, geom="point", color="red")

# Use geom_pointrange()
g + stat_summary(fun.data=mean_sdl, fun.args = list(mult=1),
                geom="pointrange", color="red")
```

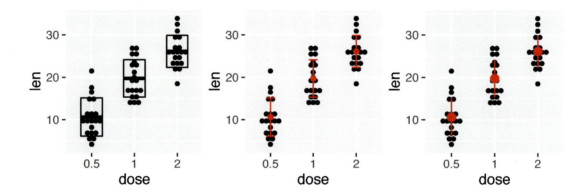

Chapter 22

Pie Charts

The function **coord_polar()** is used to produce a **pie chart**, which is just a stacked bar chart in polar coordinates.

22.1 Basic pie charts

Create some data :

```
df <- data.frame(
  group = c("Male", "Female", "Child"),
  value = c(25, 25, 50))
head(df)
```

```
##      group value
## 1   Male    25
## 2 Female    25
## 3  Child    50
```

Create a pie chart :

```
# default plot
p <- ggplot(df, aes(x="", y = value, fill=group)) +
      geom_bar(width = 1, stat = "identity") +
```

```
        coord_polar("y", start=0)
p

# Use custom fill color palettes
p + scale_fill_manual(values=c("#999999", "#E69F00", "#56B4E9"))
```

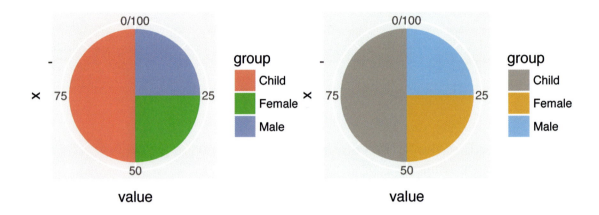

22.2   Customized pie charts

Create a blank theme :

```
blank_theme <- theme_minimal()+
  theme(
  axis.title.x = element_blank(),
  axis.title.y = element_blank(),
  axis.text.x=element_blank(),
  panel.border = element_blank(),
  panel.grid=element_blank(),
  axis.ticks = element_blank(),
  plot.title=element_text(size=14, face="bold")
  )
```

1. Apply the blank theme
2. Remove axis tick mark labels
3. Add text annotations : The package **scales** is used to format the labels in *percent*

```
# Apply blank theme
require(scales)
p + scale_fill_brewer("Blues") + blank_theme +
  geom_text(aes(y = value/3 + c(0, cumsum(value)[-length(value)]),
           label = percent(value/100)), size=5)
```

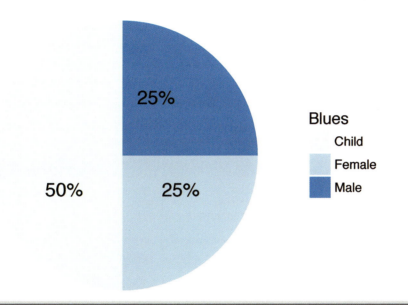

In the R code above, we used the function **scale_fill_brewer()** to change fill colors. You can read more about colors in Chapter 26

Part V

Graphical Parameters

Chapter 23

Graphical Primitives

This section describes how to add **graphical elements** (polygon, path, ribbon, segment and rectangle) to a plot.

- **Key functions**: *geom_path(), geom_ribbon(), geom_rect(), geom_segment()*

- **Key arguments to customize the plot**: *alpha, color, fill (for ribbon only), linetype and size*

The functions below we'll be used:

geom_polygon(): Add *polygon*, a filled path

geom_path(): *Connect observations* in original order

geom_ribbon(): Add *ribbons*, y range with continuous x values.

geom_segment(): Add a single line *segments*

geom_curve(): Add *curves*

geom_rect(): Add a 2d *rectangles*.

1. The R code below draws France map using **geom_polygon()**:

```
require(maps)
france = map_data('world', region = 'France')
ggplot(france, aes(x = long, y = lat, group = group)) +
  geom_polygon(fill = 'white', colour = 'black')
```

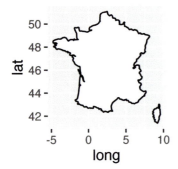

2. Use **econimics** data [in **ggplot2**] and produces **path**, **ribbon** and **rectangles**.

```
h <- ggplot(economics, aes(date, unemploy))
# Path
h + geom_path(size = 0.8, color = "#E46726") +
  theme_minimal()
```

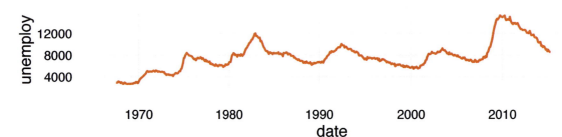

```
# Combine path, ribbon and rectangle
h + geom_rect(aes(xmin = as.Date('1980-01-01'), ymin = -Inf,
              xmax = as.Date('1985-01-01'), ymax = Inf),
          fill = "#A29B32", color = "#D8DA9E", size =1.5) +
  geom_ribbon(aes(ymin = unemploy-900, ymax = unemploy+900),
              fill = "#F3BF94") +
  geom_path(size = 0.8, color = "#E46726") +
  theme_minimal()
```

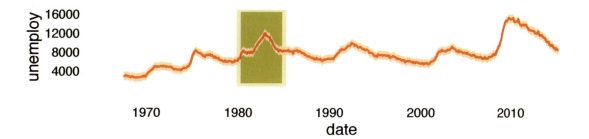

3. **Add line segments** and **curves** between points (x1, y1) and (x2, y2):

```
# Create a scatter plot
i <- ggplot(mtcars, aes(wt, mpg)) + geom_point()

# Add segment
i + geom_segment(aes(x = 2, y = 15, xend = 3, yend = 15))

# Add arrow
require(grid)
i + geom_segment(aes(x = 5, y = 30, xend = 3.5, yend = 25),
                 arrow = arrow(length = unit(0.5, "cm")))

# Add curves
i + geom_curve(aes(x = 2, y = 15, xend = 3, yend = 15))
```

Chapter 24

Main Titles, Axis Labels and Legend Title

- **Key functions**: *ggtitle(), xlab(), ylab(), labs()*

We start by creating a box plot using the data set **ToothGrowth**:

```
# Convert the variable dose from numeric to factor variable
ToothGrowth$dose <- as.factor(ToothGrowth$dose)
p <- ggplot(ToothGrowth, aes(x=dose, y=len, fill = dose)) + geom_boxplot()
```

The function below can be used for changing **titles** and **labels**:

p + ggtitle("Main title"): Adds a main title above the plot

p + xlab("X axis label"): Changes the X axis label

p + ylab("Y axis label"): Changes the Y axis label

p + labs(title = "Main title", x = "X axis label", y = "Y axis label"): Changes main title and axis labels

The function **labs()** can be also used to change the **legend title**.

24.1   Change the main title and axis labels

```r
# Default plot
print(p)

# Change title and axis labels
p <- p +labs(title="Plot of length \n by dose",
        x ="Dose (mg)", y = "Teeth length")
p
```

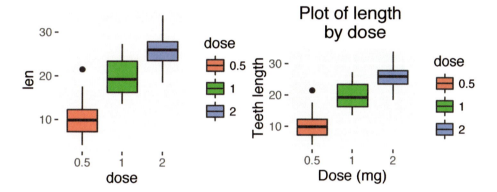

Note that, you can use \n, to split long title into multiple lines.

Plot titles can be also changed using the functions *ggtitle(), xlab(), ylab()* as follow.

```r
p + ggtitle("Plot of length \n by dose") +
  xlab("Dose (mg)") + ylab("Teeth length")
```

24.2   Change the appearance of labels

To change the appearance (**color**, **size** and **face**) of labels, the functions **theme()** and **element_text()** can be used.

The function **element_blank()** hides the labels.

```
# Change the appearance of labels.
# Values for face are one of "plain", "italic", "bold" and "bold.italic"
p + theme(
plot.title = element_text(color="red", size=12, face="bold.italic"),
axis.title.x = element_text(color="blue", size=12, face="bold"),
axis.title.y = element_text(color="#993333", size=12, face="bold")
)
# Hide labels
p + theme(plot.title = element_blank(),
          axis.title.x = element_blank(),
          axis.title.y = element_blank())
```

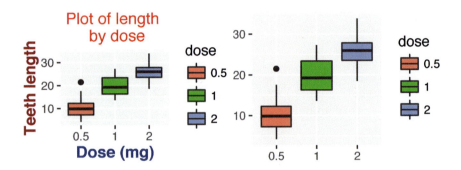

24.3   Change legend titles

labs() and scale functions (fill, color, size, shape, . . .) are used to update legend titles.

```
p + labs(fill = "Dose (mg)")
```

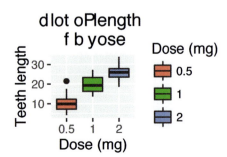

Chapter 25

Legend Position and Appearance

> • **Key functions**: *guides(), guide_legend() and guide_colourbar().*

• Create a box plot

```
# Convert the variable dose from numeric to factor variable
ToothGrowth$dose <- as.factor(ToothGrowth$dose)
p <- ggplot(ToothGrowth, aes(x=dose, y=len, fill=dose))+
  geom_boxplot()
```

25.1   Change legend position and appearance

1. Change legend position and appearance

```
# Change legend position: "left","top", "right", "bottom", "none"
p + theme(legend.position="top")

# Legend position as numeric vector c(x, y)
p + theme(legend.position = c(0.8, 0.2))
```

```
# Remove legends
p + theme(legend.position = "none")
```

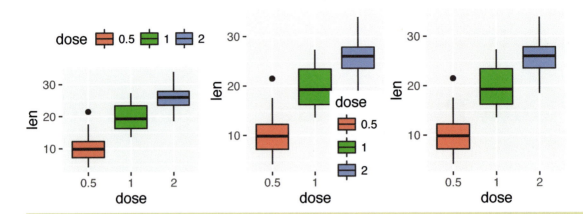

> As shown above, the argument **legend.position** can be also a numeric vector c(x,y),
> where x and y are the coordinates of the legend box. Their values should be between
> 0 and 1. c(0,0) corresponds to the "bottom left" and c(1,1) corresponds to the "top
> right" position.

```
# Change the appearance of legend title and labels
p + theme(legend.title = element_text(colour="blue"),
          legend.text = element_text(colour="red"))
```

```
# Change legend box background color
p + theme(legend.background = element_rect(fill="lightblue"))
```

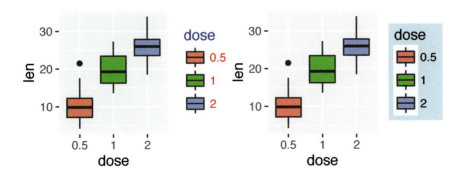

2. **Customize legends using scale functions**

- Change the order of legend items: **scale_x_discrete()**
- Set legend title and labels: **scale_fill_discrete()**

```
# Change the order of legend items
p + scale_x_discrete(limits=c("2", "0.5", "1"))
```

```
# Set legend title and labels
p + scale_fill_discrete(name = "Dose", labels = c("A", "B", "C"))
```

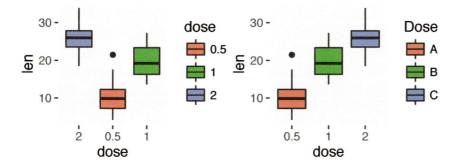

25.2 guides() : set or remove the legend for a specific aesthetic

It's possible to use the function **guides()** to set or remove the legend of a particular aesthetic (fill, color, size, shape, etc).

1. **Prepare the data**

```
# convert cyl and gear to factor variables
mtcars$cyl<-as.factor(mtcars$cyl)
mtcars$gear <- as.factor(mtcars$gear)
```

2. **Create a scatter plot with multiple aesthetics (guides)**

The color and the shape of the points are determined by the factor variables *cyl* and *gear*, respectively. The size of the points are controlled by the variable qsec.

The function **guide_legend()** is used to change the order of guides.

```
# Plot with multiple aesthetics
p <- ggplot(data = mtcars,
    aes(x = mpg, y = wt, color = cyl, size = qsec, shape = gear))+
    geom_point()
p

# Change the order of guides using guide_legend()
p + guides(color = guide_legend(order=1),
        size = guide_legend(order=2),
        shape = guide_legend(order=3))

# Remove a legend for a particular aesthetic (color and size)
p+guides(color = FALSE, size = FALSE)
```

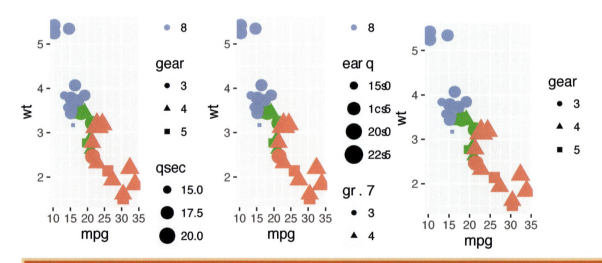

Note that, in the case of continuous color, the function **guide_colourbar**() should be used to change the order of color guide.

```
# Case of continuous color: Use guide_colourbar()
qplot(data = mpg, x = displ, y = cty, size = hwy,
      colour = cyl, shape = drv) +
  guides(colour = guide_colourbar(order = 1),
        alpha = guide_legend(order = 2),
        size = guide_legend(order = 3))
```

Removing a particular legend can be done also when using the functions **scale_xx**. In this case the argument *guide* is used as follow.

```
# Remove legend for the point shape
p + scale_shape(guide=FALSE)
# Remove legend for size
p + scale_size(guide=FALSE)
# Remove legend for color
p + scale_color_manual(values=c('#999999','#E69F00','#56B4E9'),
                       guide=FALSE)
```

Chapter 26

Colors

This chapter describes how to change the **color** of a graph. A color can be specified either by name (e.g.: "red") or by hexadecimal code (e.g. : "#FF1234").

You will learn how to :

- change colors by groups (automatically and manually)
- use RColorBrewer and Wes Anderson color palettes
- use gradient colors

ToothGrowth and *mtcars* data sets are used in the examples below.

```
# Convert dose and cyl columns from numeric to factor variables
ToothGrowth$dose <- as.factor(ToothGrowth$dose)
mtcars$cyl <- as.factor(mtcars$cyl)
```

We start by creating some plots which will be finished hereafter:

```
# Box plot
bp <- ggplot(ToothGrowth, aes(x=dose, y=len))

# Scatter plot
sp <- ggplot(mtcars, aes(x=wt, y=mpg))
```

26.1 Use a single color

Change fill and outline colors

```
# box plot
bp + geom_boxplot(fill = 'steelblue', color = "red")
```

```
# scatter plot
sp + geom_point(color = 'darkblue')
```

26.2 Change colors by groups

1. **Changes colors by groups** using the levels of *dose* variable :

```
# Box plot
bp <- bp + geom_boxplot(aes(fill = dose))
bp
```

```
# Scatter plot
sp <- sp + geom_point(aes(color = cyl))
sp
```

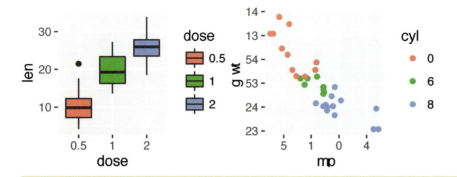

The lightness (l) and the chroma (c, intensity of color) of the default (hue) colors can be modified using the functions *scale_hue* as follow.

```
# Box plot
bp + scale_fill_hue(l=40, c=35)
```

```
# Scatter plot
sp + scale_color_hue(l=40, c=35)
```

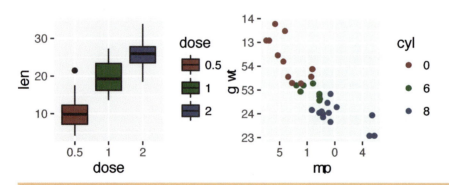

Note that, the default values for l and c are : l = 65, c = 100.

2. **Change colors manually** usin a custom color palettes:

  - **scale_fill_manual()** for box plot, bar plot, violin plot, dot plot, etc
  - **scale_color_manual()** for lines and points

```
# Box plot
bp + scale_fill_manual(values=c("#999999", "#E69F00", "#56B4E9"))

# Scatter plot
sp + scale_color_manual(values=c("#999999", "#E69F00", "#56B4E9"))
```

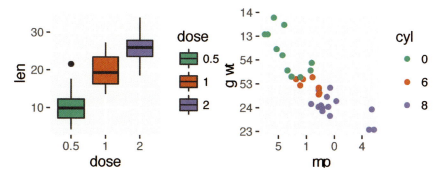

3. **Use RColorBrewer palettes**

- **scale_fill_brewer**() for box plot, bar plot, violin plot, dot plot, etc
- **scale_color_brewer**() for lines and points

```
# Box plot
bp + scale_fill_brewer(palette="Dark2")

# Scatter plot
sp + scale_color_brewer(palette="Dark2")
```

The available color palettes in the RColorBrewer package are :

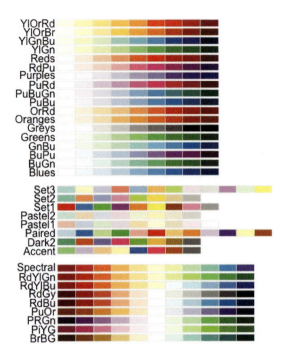

4. Use Wes Anderson color palettes

Install and load the color palettes as follow :

```r
# Install
install.packages("wesanderson")
# Load
library(wesanderson)
```

The available color palettes are :

```r
library(wesanderson)
# Box plot
bp+scale_fill_manual(values=wes_palette(n=3, name="GrandBudapest"))

# Scatter plot
sp+scale_color_manual(values=wes_palette(n=3, name="GrandBudapest"))
```

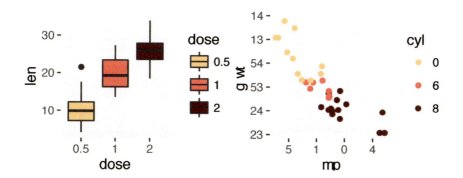

5. **Use gray color palettes**:

- scale__fill__grey() for box plot, bar plot, violin plot, dot plot, etc
- scale__colour__grey() for points, lines, etc

```r
# Box plot
bp + scale_fill_grey(start=0.8, end=0.2) + theme_minimal()

# Scatter plot
sp + scale_color_grey(start=0.8, end=0.2) + theme_minimal()
```

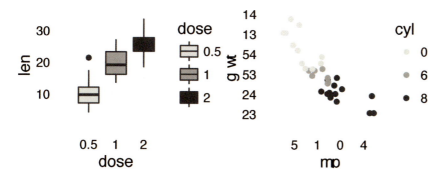

26.3   Gradient or continuous colors

Plots can be colored according to the values of a continuous variable using the functions
:

- **scale_color_gradient**(), **scale_fill_gradient**() for sequential gradients between two colors
- **scale_color_gradient2**(), **scale_fill_gradient2**() for diverging gradients
- **scale_color_gradientn**(), **scale_fill_gradientn**() for gradient between n colors

26.3.1   Gradient between two colors

The graphs are colored using the *qsec* continuous variable :

```
# Color by qsec values
sp2 <- ggplot(mtcars, aes(x = wt, y = mpg)) +
    geom_point(aes(color = qsec))
sp2

# Change the low and high colors
# Sequential color scheme
sp2+scale_color_gradient(low="blue", high="red")

# Diverging color scheme
mid <- mean(mtcars$qsec)
sp2 + scale_color_gradient2(midpoint = mid, low = "blue", mid = "white",
                            high = "red", space = "Lab" )
```

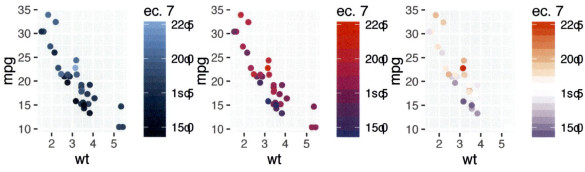

Note that, the functions **scale_color_continuous()** and **scale_fill_continuous()** can be used also to set gradient colors.

26.3.2 Gradient between n colors

```
# Scatter plot
# Color points by the mpg variable
sp3 <- ggplot(mtcars, aes(x = wt, y = mpg)) +
  geom_point(aes(color = mpg))
sp3

# Gradient between n colors
sp3 + scale_color_gradientn(colours = rainbow(5))
```

Chapter 27

Point Shapes, colors and size

The different **points shapes** commonly used in **R** are illustrated in the figure below :

0	1	2	3	4
□	○	△	+	×

5	6	7	8	9
◇	▽	⊠	✳	⊕

10	11	12	13	14
⊕	⋈	⊞	⊠	◩

15	16	17	18	19
■	●	▲	◆	●

20	21	22	23	24	25
•	●	■	◆	▲	▼

mtcars data is used in the following examples.

```
# Convert cyl as factor variable
mtcars$cyl <- as.factor(mtcars$cyl)
```

Create a scatter plot and change point shapes, colors and size:

```r
# Change shape, color and size
ggplot(mtcars, aes(x = wt, y = mpg)) +
  geom_point(shape = 18, color = "steelblue", size = 4)

# change shape, color, fill, size
ggplot(mtcars, aes(x = wt, y = mpg)) +
  geom_point(shape = 23, fill = "blue",
             color = "darkred", size = 3)

# Change point shapes and colors by groups
ggplot(mtcars, aes(x = wt, y = mpg)) +
  geom_point(aes(shape = cyl, color = cyl))

# Control the size by groups
# ggplot(mtcars, aes(x = wt, y = mpg)) +
#  geom_point(aes(size = cyl))
```

Note that, the argument **fill** can be used only for the point shapes 21 to 25.

It's also possible to manually change the appearance of points:

- **scale_shape_manual()** : to change point shapes
- **scale_color_manual()** : to change point colors
- **scale_size_manual()** : to change the size of points

```
# Change colors and shapes manually
ggplot(mtcars, aes(x=wt, y=mpg, group=cyl)) +
  geom_point(aes(shape=cyl, color=cyl), size=2)+
  scale_shape_manual(values=c(3, 16, 17))+
  scale_color_manual(values=c('#999999','#E69F00', '#56B4E9'))+
  theme(legend.position="top")

# Change the point size manually
ggplot(mtcars, aes(x=wt, y=mpg, group=cyl)) +
  geom_point(aes(shape=cyl, color=cyl, size=cyl))+
  scale_shape_manual(values=c(3, 16, 17))+
  scale_color_manual(values=c('#999999','#E69F00', '#56B4E9'))+
  scale_size_manual(values=c(1.5,2,3))+
  theme(legend.position="top")
```

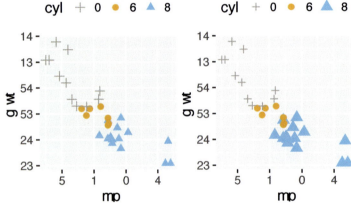

Chapter 28

Line types

The different line types available in **R software** are : **"blank"**, **"solid"**, **"dashed"**, **"dotted"**, **"dotdash"**, **"longdash"**, **"twodash"**.

> Note that, line types can be also specified using numbers : **0, 1, 2, 3, 4, 5, 6**. 0 is for "blank", 1 is for "solid", 2 is for "dashed", ...

A graph of the different line types is shown below :

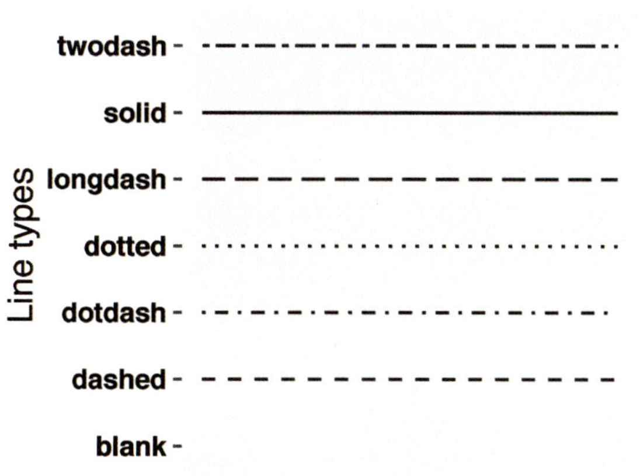

1. **Basic line plot**

```
# Create some data
df <- data.frame(time=c("breakfeast", "Lunch", "Dinner"),
                 bill=c(10, 30, 15))
head(df)
```

```
##           time bill
## 1 breakfeast   10
## 2      Lunch   30
## 3      Dinner   15
```

```r
# Basic line plot with points
# Change the line type
ggplot(data = df, aes(x = time, y = bill, group = 1)) +
  geom_line(linetype = "dashed")+
  geom_point()
```

2. Line plot with multiple groups

```r
# Create some data
df2 <- data.frame(sex = rep(c("Female", "Male"), each=3),
                  time=c("breakfeast", "Lunch", "Dinner"),
                  bill=c(10, 30, 15, 13, 40, 17) )
head(df2)
```

```
##        sex       time bill
## 1 Female breakfeast   10
## 2 Female      Lunch   30
## 3 Female      Dinner   15
## 4   Male breakfeast   13
## 5   Male      Lunch   40
## 6   Male      Dinner   17
```

```
# Line plot with multiple groups
# Change line types and colors by groups (sex)
ggplot(df2, aes(x=time, y=bill, group=sex)) +
  geom_line(aes(linetype = sex, color = sex))+
  geom_point(aes(color=sex))
```

The functions below can be used to change the appearance of line types manually:

- **scale_linetype_manual()** : to change line types
- **scale_color_manual()** : to change line colors
- **scale_size_manual()** : to change the size of lines

```
# Change line types, colors and sizes
ggplot(df2, aes(x=time, y=bill, group=sex)) +
  geom_line(aes(linetype=sex, color=sex, size=sex))+
  geom_point()+
  scale_linetype_manual(values=c("twodash", "dotted"))+
  scale_color_manual(values=c('#999999','#E69F00'))+
  scale_size_manual(values=c(1, 1.5))
```

Chapter 29

Axis limits: Minimum and Maximum values

There are different functions for setting axis limits:

1. **Without clipping (preferred):**

   - p + **coord_cartesian**(xlim = c(5, 20), ylim = (0, 50)): **Cartesian coordinates**. The Cartesian coordinate system is the most common type of coordinate system. It will zoom the plot (like you're looking at it with a magnifying glass), without clipping the data.

2. **With clipping the data**: (removes unseen data points): Observations not in this range will be dropped completely and not passed to any other layers.

   - p + **xlim**(5, 20) + **ylim**(0, 50)
   - p + **scale_x_continuous**(limits = c(5, 20)) + **scale_y_continuous**(limits = c(0, 50))

3. **Expand the plot limits with data**: This function is a thin wrapper around **geom_blank()** that makes it easy to add data to a plot.

   - p + **expand_limits**(x = 0, y = 0): set the intercept of x and y axes at (0,0)
   - p + **expand_limits**(x = c(5, 50), y = c(0, 150))

We start by creating a plot using **cars** data set:

```
data(cars)
p <- ggplot(cars, aes(x = speed, y = dist)) + geom_point()
```

1. Use coord_cartesian(), xlim(), ylim() and expand_limits():

```
# Default plot
print(p)
```

```
# Change axis limits using coord_cartesian()
p + coord_cartesian(xlim =c(5, 20), ylim = c(0, 50))
```

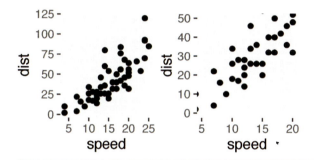

Note that, the function **expand_limits()** can be also used to quickly set the intercept of x and y axes at (0,0).

```
# set the intercept of x and y axis at (0,0)
p + expand_limits(x = 0, y=0)
```

2. **Use scale_x_x() functions**: The functions *scale_x_continuous()* and *scale_y_continuous()* can be used to change x and y axis limits/labels, respectively:

```
# Change x and y axis labels, and limits
p + scale_x_continuous(name="Speed of cars", limits=c(0, 30)) +
  scale_y_continuous(name="Stopping distance", limits=c(0, 150))
```

Chapter 30

Axis transformations: log and sqrt

1. **Create a scatter plot:**

```
data(cars)
p <- ggplot(cars, aes(x = speed, y = dist)) + geom_point()
```

2. **Functions for continuous axis transformations:**

- p + **scale_x_log10()**, p + **scale_y_log10()** : Plot x and y on **log10** scale, respectively.

- p + **scale_x_sqrt()**, p + **scale_y_sqrt()** : Plot x and y on **square root** scale, respectively.

- p + **scale_x_reverse()**, p + **scale_y_reverse()** : Reverse direction of axes

- p + **coord_trans**(x ="log10", y="log10") : transformed cartesian coordinate system. Possible values for x and y are "log2", "log10", "sqrt", ...

- p + **scale_x_continuous**(trans='log2'), p + **scale_y_continuous**(trans='log2') : another allowed value for the argument *trans* is 'log10'

3. Use the function **scale_xx_continuous()** to transform axis scales:

```
# Default scatter plot
print(p)

# Log transformation using scale_xx()
# possible values for trans : 'log2', 'log10','sqrt'
p + scale_x_continuous(trans='log2') +
  scale_y_continuous(trans='log2')

# Format axis tick mark labels to show exponents
require(scales)
p + scale_y_continuous(trans = log2_trans(),
    breaks = trans_breaks("log2", function(x) 2^x),
    labels = trans_format("log2", math_format(2^.x)))

# Reverse coordinates
p + scale_y_reverse()
```

4. **Format axis tick mark labels**: The **scales** package is required to access break formatting functions.

```
require(scales)
# Percent
p + scale_y_continuous(labels = percent)

# Dollar
p + scale_y_continuous(labels = dollar)

# Scientific
p + scale_y_continuous(labels = scientific)
```

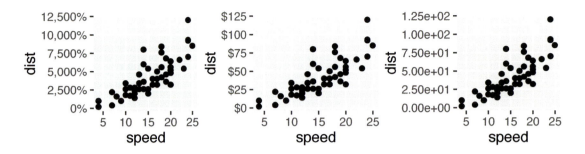

5. **Display log tick marks**: the function **annotation_logticks()** will be used.

> Note that, these tick marks make sense only for base 10.

Data: *Animals* data sets, from the package *MASS*.

```r
# Required package
require(MASS) # to access Animals data sets
require(scales) # to access break formatting functions
data(Animals) # Load data

# x and y axis are transformed and formatted
p2 <- ggplot(Animals, aes(x = body, y = brain)) + geom_point() +
    scale_x_log10(breaks = trans_breaks("log10", function(x) 10^x),
            labels = trans_format("log10", math_format(10^.x))) +
    scale_y_log10(breaks = trans_breaks("log10", function(x) 10^x),
            labels = trans_format("log10", math_format(10^.x))) +
    theme_bw()

# log-log plot without log tick marks
p2

# Show log tick marks
p2 + annotation_logticks()
```

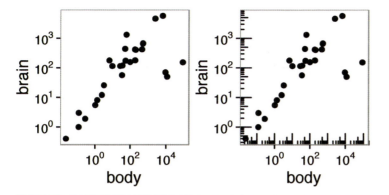

Note that, default log ticks are on bottom and left.

To specify the sides of the log ticks :

```r
# Log ticks on left and right
p2 + annotation_logticks(sides="lr")

# All sides
p2+annotation_logticks(sides="trbl")
```

Allowed values for the argument *sides* are the combination of "t"(top), "r"(right), "b"(bottom), "l"(left).

Chapter 31

Date Axes

The functions **scale_x_date**() and **scale_y_date**() are used to format date axes. Create some time series data sets:

```
set.seed(1234)
df <- data.frame(
  date = seq(Sys.Date(), len=100, by="1 day")[sample(100, 50)],
  price = runif(50)
)
df <- df[order(df$date), ]
head(df)
```

```
##           date      price
## 7   2016-04-21 0.49396092
## 24  2016-04-24 0.78312110
## 1   2016-05-02 0.07377988
## 23  2016-05-03 0.01462726
## 19  2016-05-06 0.05164662
## 25  2016-05-07 0.08996133
```

31.1 Format axis tick mark labels: days, weeks, months

The R package **scales** is required.

```r
# Default plot
p <- ggplot(data=df, aes(x = date, y=price)) + geom_line()
p

# Format axis tick mark labels
# Format : month/day
require(scales)
p + scale_x_date(labels = date_format("%m/%d")) +
  theme(axis.text.x = element_text(angle=45))

# Format : Week
p + scale_x_date(labels = date_format("%W"))

# Months only
p + scale_x_date(breaks = date_breaks("months"),
  labels = date_format("%b")) +
  theme(axis.text.x = element_text(angle=45))
```

31.2   Date axis limits

US economic time series data sets are used :

```
# Plot with dates
data("economics")
p <- ggplot(data = economics, aes(x = date, y = psavert)) +
    geom_line(color = "steelblue")
p

# Axis limits c(min, max)
min <- as.Date("2002-1-1")
max <- max(economics$date)
p + scale_x_date(limits = c(min, max))
```

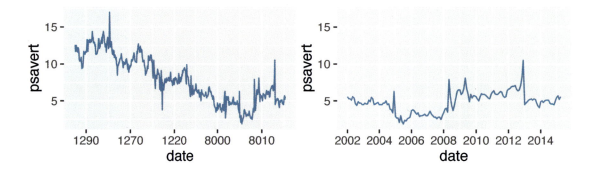

Chapter 32

Axis Ticks : Customize Tick Marks and Labels, Reorder and Select items

1. Functions for changing the style of axis tick mark labels:

- **element_text**(face, color, size, angle): change text style -

- element_blank(): Hide text

2. Create a box plot:

```
data("ToothGrowth")
ToothGrowth$dose <- as.factor(ToothGrowth$dose)
p <- ggplot(ToothGrowth, aes(x=dose, y=len)) + geom_boxplot()
# print(p)
```

3. Change the style and the orientation angle of axis tick labels

```
# Change the style of axis tick labels
# face can be "plain", "italic", "bold" or "bold.italic"
p + theme(axis.text.x = element_text(face="bold", color="#993333",
                            size=12, angle=45),
          axis.text.y = element_text(face="bold", color="blue",
                            size=12, angle=45))
```

```
# Remove axis ticks and tick mark labels
p + theme(
  axis.text.x = element_blank(), # Remove x axis tick labels
  axis.text.y = element_blank(), # Remove y axis tick labels
  axis.ticks = element_blank()) # Remove ticks
```

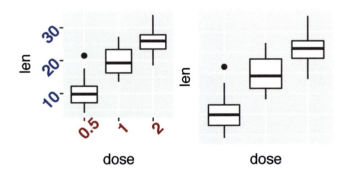

4. **Change axis lines**: the function **element_line()** is used.

```
# Change the line type and color of axis lines
p + theme( axis.line = element_line(colour = "darkblue",
                        size = 1, linetype = "solid"))
```

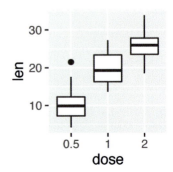

5. Customize continuous and discrete axes

x or y axis can be discrete or continuous. In each of these two cases, the functions to be used for setting axis ticks are different.

- **Discrete axes**

    - **scale_x_discrete**(name, breaks, labels, limits): for X axis
    - **scale_y_discrete**(name, breaks, labels, limits): for y axis

- **Continuous axes**

    - **scale_x_continuous**(name, breaks, labels, limits, trans): for X axis
    - **scale_y_continuous**(name, breaks, labels, limits, trans): for y axis

Briefly, the meaning of the arguments are as follow:

- **name** : x or y axis labels

- **breaks** : vector specifying which breaks to display

- **labels** : labels of axis tick marks

- **limits** : vector indicating the data range

scale_xx() functions can be used to change the following x or y axis parameters :

- axis titles
- axis limits (data range to display)
- choose where tick marks appear
- manually label tick marks

5.1. Discrete axes

Note that, in the examples below, we'll use only the functions **scale_x_discrete()** and **xlim()** to customize x axis tick marks. The same kind of examples can be applied to a discrete y axis using the functions **scale_y_discrete()** and **ylim()**.

```
# Default plot
print(p)

# Change x axis label and the order of items
p + scale_x_discrete(name ="Dose (mg)",
                     limits=c("2","1","0.5"))

# Change tick mark labels
p + scale_x_discrete(breaks=c("0.5","1","2"),
        labels=c("D0.5", "D1", "D2"))

# Choose which items to display
p + scale_x_discrete(limits=c("0.5", "2"))

# or use this:
# p + xlim("0.5", "2") # same as above
```

5.2 Continuous axes

```
# Default scatter plot
sp <- ggplot(cars, aes(x = speed, y = dist)) + geom_point()
sp


# Change x and y axis labels, and limits
sp + scale_x_continuous(name="Speed of cars", limits=c(0, 30)) +
  scale_y_continuous(name="Stopping distance", limits=c(0, 150))

#  Set tick marks on y axis: a tick mark is shown on every 50
sp + scale_y_continuous(breaks=seq(0, 150, 50))
```

```
# Tick marks can be spaced randomly
sp + scale_y_continuous(breaks=c(0, 50, 65, 75, 150))

# Remove tick mark labels and gridlines
sp + scale_y_continuous(breaks=NULL)

# Format the labels
# ++++++++++++++++++
require(scales)
# Possible values for labels = percent, scientific, ..
sp + scale_y_continuous(labels = percent) # labels as percents
```

Possible values for labels are comma, percent, dollar and scientific. For more examples, read the documentation of the function trans_new() in *scales* package

Chapter 33

Themes and Background Colors

This chapter describes how to change the look of a plot **theme** (*background color*, *panel background color* and *grid lines*). You'll also learn how to use ggplot2 base themes to create your own theme.

ToothGrowth data will be used :

```
data("ToothGrowth")
# Convert the column dose from numeric to factor variable
ToothGrowth$dose <- as.factor(ToothGrowth$dose)
```

We start by creating a simple box plot:

```
p <- ggplot(ToothGrowth, aes(x=dose, y=len)) +
  geom_boxplot()
```

33.1   Change plot themes: Quick functions

Several functions are available in ggplot2 package for changing quickly the theme of plots :

theme_gray(): gray background color and white grid lines

theme_bw(): white background and gray grid lines

theme_linedraw(): black lines around the plot

theme_light(): light gray lines and axis (more attention towards the data)

```
p + theme_gray(base_size = 14)
```

```
p + theme_bw()
```

```
p + theme_linedraw()
```

```
p + theme_light()
```

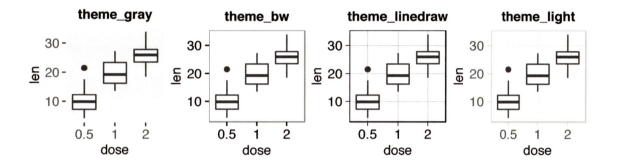

theme_minimal(): no background annotations

theme_classic(): theme with axis lines and no grid lines (standard plot)

theme_void(): Empty theme, useful for plots with non-standard coordinates or for drawings

theme_dark(): Dark background designed to make colours pop out

```
p + theme_minimal()
```

```
p + theme_minimal()
```

```
p + theme_void()
```

```
p + theme_dark()
```

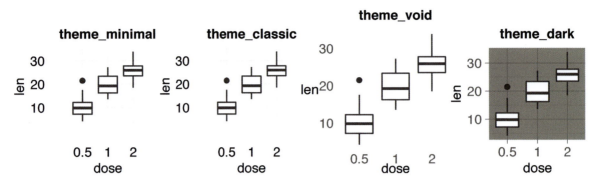

The functions theme_xx() can take the two arguments below :

- **base_size** : base font size (to change the size of all plot text elements)

- **base_family** : base font family

The size of all the plot text elements can be easily changed at once :

```
# Example 1
p + theme_gray(base_size = 10)

# Example 2
p + theme_gray(base_size = 20)
```

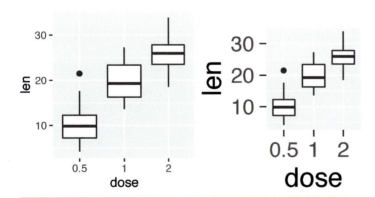

> Note that, the function **theme_set()** can be used to change the theme for the entire session.

```
theme_set(theme_gray(base_size = 20))
```

33.2   Customize plot background

The function **theme()** is used to control non-data parts of the graph including :

- **Line elements:** axis lines, minor and major grid lines, plot panel border, axis ticks background color, etc.

- **Text elements:** plot title, axis titles, legend title and text, axis tick mark labels, etc.

- **Rectangle elements:** plot background, panel background, legend background, etc.

There is a specific function to modify each of these three elements :

element_line() to modify the line elements of the theme

element_text() to modify the text elements

element_rect() to change the appearance of the rectangle elements

> Note that, each of the theme elements can be removed using the function **element_blank()**

33.2.1   Change colors

In this section we'll change the color of the plot panel background and the grid lines.

- The functions **theme()** and **element_rect(fill, colour, size, linetype)** are used for changing the plot panel background color.

- The appearance of **grid lines** can be changed using the function **element_line(colour, size, linetype)**.

```r
# Change the colors of plot panel background to lightblue
# and the color of major/grid lines to white
p + theme(
  panel.background = element_rect(fill = "#BFD5E3", colour = "#6D9EC1",
                                  size = 2, linetype = "solid"),
  panel.grid.major = element_line(size = 0.5, linetype = 'solid',
                                  colour = "white"),
  panel.grid.minor = element_line(size = 0.25, linetype = 'solid',
                                  colour = "white")
  )

# Change the plot background color
p + theme(plot.background = element_rect(fill = "#BFD5E3"))
```

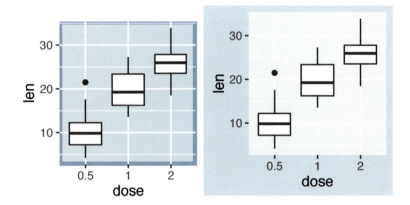

33.2.2 Remove panel borders and grid lines

It is possible to hide plot panel borders and grid lines with the function **element_blank()** as follow :

```r
# Hide panel borders and grid lines
# But change axis line
p + theme(panel.border = element_blank(),
          panel.grid.major = element_blank(),
          panel.grid.minor = element_blank(),
          axis.line = element_line(size = 0.5, linetype = "solid",
                                   colour = "black"))
```

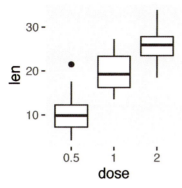

33.3   Use ggthemes

You can change the entire appearance of a plot by using a custom theme. Jeffrey Arnold has implemented the library **ggthemes** containing several custom themes.

Read more about **ggthemes**: https://github.com/jrnold/ggthemes

To use these themes install and load ggthemes package as follow :

```r
install.packages("ggthemes") # Install
library(ggthemes) # Load
```

ggthemes package provides many custom themes and scales. Two of themes are shown below:

```r
p <- ggplot(ToothGrowth, aes(x = dose, y = len)) +
  geom_boxplot(aes(fill = dose))
# theme_economist
p + theme_economist() + scale_fill_economist()

# theme_stata
p + theme_stata() + scale_fill_stata()
```

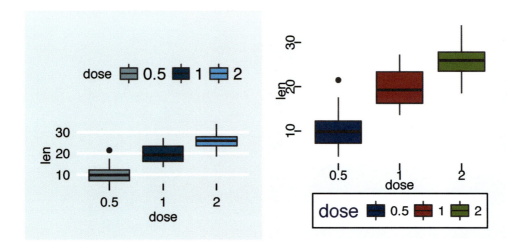

33.4   Create your theme

1. You can change the theme for the current R session using the function theme_set() as follow :

```
theme_set(theme_gray(base_size = 20))
```

2. You can extract and modify the R code of theme_gray :

```
theme_gray

function (base_size = 11, base_family = "") {
 half_line <- base_size/2
theme(
  ...
  axis.text = element_text(size = rel(0.8), colour = "grey30"),
  ...
 )
}
```

> Note that, the function **rel()** modifies the size relative to the base size.

Chapter 34

Text Annotations

This article describes how to **add a text** annotation to a plot generated using **ggplot2** package.

The functions below can be used :

- **geom_text**(): adds text directly to the plot
- **geom_label**(): draws a rectangle underneath the text, making it easier to read.
- **annotate**(): useful for adding small text annotations at a particular location on the plot
- **annotation_custom**(): Adds static annotations that are the same in every panel

It's also possible to use the R package **ggrepel**, which is an extension and provides **geom** for ggplot2 to repel **overlapping text** labels away from each other.

> We'll start by describing how to use ggplot2 official functions for adding text annotations. In the last sections, examples using **ggrepel** extensions are provided.

A subset of **mtcars** data is used:

```
set.seed(1234)
df <- mtcars[sample(1:nrow(mtcars), 10), ]
df$cyl <- as.factor(df$cyl)
```

34.1   Text annotations using geom_text and geom_label

```
# Simple scatter plot
sp <- ggplot(df, aes(wt, mpg, label = rownames(df)))+
  geom_point()

# Add text, change colors by groups
# Change vertical justification
sp + geom_text(aes(label = rownames(df), color = cyl),
               size = 3, vjust = -1)

# Add text at a particular coordinate
sp + geom_text(x = 3, y = 30, label = "Scatter plot",
               color="red", fontface = 2)
```

> **geom_label()** works like **geom_text()** but draws a rounded rectangle underneath each label. This is useful when you want to label plots that are dense with data.

```
sp + geom_label()
```

Others useful arguments for **geom_text()** and **geom_label()** are:

- **nudge_x** and **nudge_y**: let you offset labels from their corresponding points. The function **position_nudge()** can be also used.

- **check_overlap** = TRUE: for avoiding overplotting of labels

- **hjust** and **vjust** can now be character vectors (ggplot2 v >= 2.0.0): "left", "center", "right", "bottom", "middle", "top". New options include "inward" and "outward" which align text towards and away from the center of the plot respectively.

- **fontface**: Change fontface. Allowed values : 1 (normal), 2 (bold), 3 (italic) and 4 (bold.italic).

34.2 annotation_custom : Add a static text annotation

The functions **annotation_custom()** and **textGrob()** are used to add static annotations which are the same in every panel. The *grid* package is required :

```
# Create a scatter plot
sp2 <- ggplot(mtcars, aes(x=wt, y=mpg, label=rownames(mtcars)))+
geom_point()

#  Create a static text annotation
library(grid)
grob <- grobTree(textGrob("Scatter plot", x=0.1,  y=0.95, hjust=0,
  gp=gpar(col="red", fontsize=13, fontface="italic")))
# Plot
sp2 + annotation_custom(grob) +
  facet_wrap(~cyl, scales="free")
```

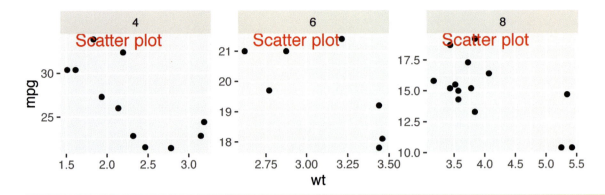

Case of **facet** (Chapter 37): the annotation is at the same place (in each facet) even if the axis scales vary.

34.3   ggrepel: Avoid overlapping of text labels

Install **ggrepel** package as follow:

```r
install.packages("ggrepel")
```

There are two important functions in **ggrepel** R packages:

- **geom_label_repel**()
- **geom_text_repel**()

We start by creating a simple scatter plot using a subset of the *mtcars* data set containing 15 rows.

1. **Prepare some data:**

```r
# Take a subset of 15 random points
set.seed(1234)
ss <- sample(1:32, 15)
df <- mtcars[ss, ]
```

2. Create a scatter plot:

```r
p <- ggplot(df, aes(wt, mpg)) +
  geom_point(color = 'red') +
  theme_minimal(base_size = 10)
```

3. Add text labels:

```r
# Add text annotations using ggplot2::geom_text
p + geom_text(aes(label = rownames(df)),
              size = 3.5)
```

```r
# Use ggrepel::geom_text_repel
require("ggrepel")
set.seed(42)
p + geom_text_repel(aes(label = rownames(df)),
                    size = 3.5)
```

```
# Use ggrepel::geom_label_repel and
# Change color by groups
set.seed(42)
p + geom_label_repel(aes(label = rownames(df),
                  fill = factor(cyl)), color = 'white',
                  size = 3.5) +
   theme(legend.position = "bottom")
```

Chapter 35

Add Straight Lines to a Plot: Horizontal, Vertical and Regression Lines

The R function below can be used :

- **geom_hline**(yintercept, linetype, color, size): for horizontal lines
- **geom_vline**(xintercept, linetype, color, size): for vertical lines
- **geom_abline**(intercept, slope, linetype, color, size): for regression lines
- **geom_segment**() to add segments

1. **Creating a simple scatter plot**

```
# Simple scatter plot
sp <- ggplot(data = mtcars, aes(x = wt, y = mpg)) + geom_point()
```

2. **Add straight lines and segments**

```
# Add horizontal line at y = 20; change line type and color
sp + geom_hline(yintercept=20, linetype="dashed", color = "red")

# Add vertical line at x = 3; change line type, color and size
```

```r
sp + geom_vline(xintercept = 3, color = "blue", size=1.5)

# Add regression line
sp + geom_abline(intercept = 37, slope = -5, color="blue")+
  ggtitle("y = -5X + 37")

# Add a vertical line segment
sp + geom_segment(aes(x = 4, y = 15, xend = 4, yend = 27))



# Add horizontal line segment
sp + geom_segment(aes(x = 2, y = 15, xend = 3, yend = 15))

# Add arrow at the end of the segment
require(grid)
sp + geom_segment(aes(x = 5, y = 30, xend = 3.5, yend = 25),
                  arrow = arrow(length = unit(0.5, "cm")))
```

Chapter 36

Rotate a Plot: Flip and Reverse

To rotate a plot, the function below can be used:

coord_flip(): Create *horizontal plots*

scale_x_reverse(), scale_y_reverse(): Reverse the axes

```
set.seed(1234)
# Basic histogram
hp <- qplot(x=rnorm(200), geom="histogram")
hp
# Horizontal histogram
hp + coord_flip()
# Y axis reversed
hp + scale_y_reverse()
```

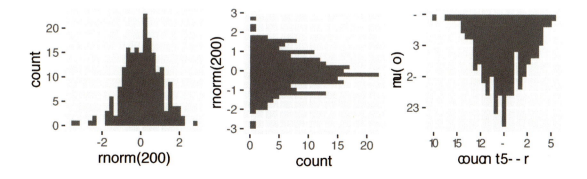

Chapter 37

Facets: Split a Plot into a Matrix of Panels

Facets divide a plot into subplots based on the values of one or more categorical variables. There are two main functions for faceting :

- **facet_grid()**
- **facet_wrap()**

Create a box plot filled by groups:

```r
# Load data and convert dose to a factor variable
data("ToothGrowth")
ToothGrowth$dose <- as.factor(ToothGrowth$dose)
# Box plot
p <- ggplot(ToothGrowth, aes(x=dose, y=len, group=dose)) +
  geom_boxplot(aes(fill=dose))
p
```

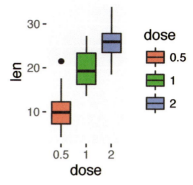

The following functions can be used for facets:

p + facet_grid(supp ~.): Facet in vertical direction based on the levels of *supp* variable.

p + facet_grid(.~supp): Facet in horizontal direction based on the levels of *supp* variable.

p + facet_grid(dose ~supp) Facet in horizontal and vertical directions based on two variables: *dose* and *supp*.

p + facet_wrap(~fl) Place facet side by side into a rectangular layout

1. **Facet with one discrete variable**: Split by the levels of the group "supp"

```
# Split in vertical direction
p + facet_grid(supp ~ .)
```

```
# Split in horizontal direction
p + facet_grid(. ~ supp)
```

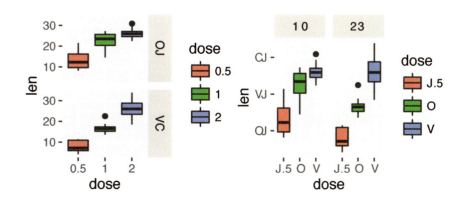

2. **Facet with two discrete variables**: Split by the levels of the groups "dose" and "supp"

```
# Facet by two variables: dose and supp.
# Rows are dose and columns are supp
p + facet_grid(dose ~ supp)

# Facet by two variables: reverse the order of the 2 variables
# Rows are supp and columns are dose
p + facet_grid(supp ~ dose)
```

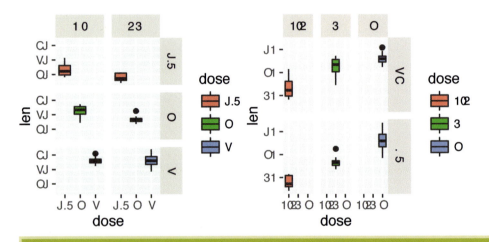

> Note that, you can use the argument *margins* to add additional facets which contain all the data for each of the possible values of the faceting variables

```
p + facet_grid(dose ~ supp, margins=TRUE)
```

3. **Facet scales**

By default, all the panels have the same scales (**scales="fixed"**). They can be made independent, by setting scales to *free, free_x,* or *free_y.*

```
p + facet_grid(dose ~ supp, scales='free')
```

4. **Facet labels**: The argument *labeller* can be used to control the labels of the panels.

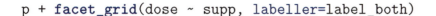

```
p + facet_grid(dose ~ supp, labeller=label_both)
```

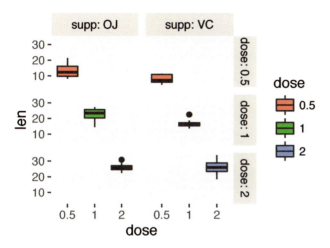

The appearance of facet labels can be modified as follow :

```
# Change facet text font. Possible values for the font style:
#'plain', 'italic', 'bold', 'bold.italic'.
p + facet_grid(dose ~ supp)+
    theme(strip.text.x = element_text(size=12, color="red",
                                      face="bold.italic"),
          strip.text.y = element_text(size=12, color="red",
                                      face="bold.italic"))
```

```
# Change the apperance of the rectangle around facet label
p + facet_grid(dose ~ supp)+
  theme(strip.background = element_rect(colour="black", fill="white",
                                        size=1.5, linetype="solid"))
```

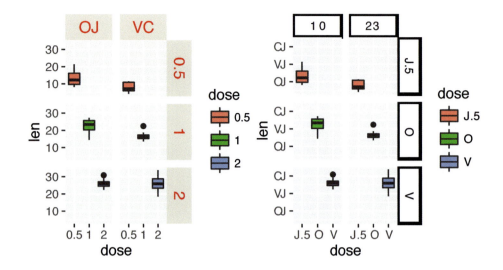

5. **facet_wrap**: Facets can be placed side by side using the function **facet_wrap()** as follow :

```
bp + facet_wrap(~ dose)
```

```
bp + facet_wrap(~ dose, ncol=2)
```

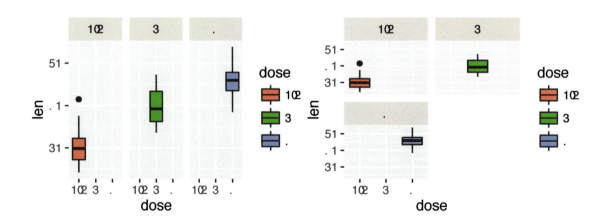

Chapter 38

Position Adjustements

Position adjustments determine how to arrange geoms. The argument **position** is used to adjust geom positions:

```
p <- ggplot(mpg, aes(fl, fill = drv))

# Arrange elements side by side
p + geom_bar(position = "dodge")

# Stack objects on top of one another,
# and normalize to have equal height
p + geom_bar(position = "fill")
```

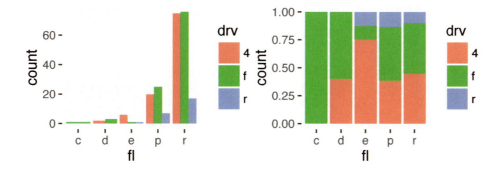

```
# Stack elements on top of one another
p + geom_bar(position = "stack")
```

```
# Add random noise to X and Y position
# of each element to avoid overplotting
ggplot(mpg, aes(cty, hwy)) +
  geom_point(position = "jitter")
```

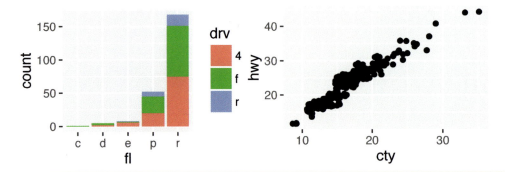

> Note that, each of these position adjustments can be done using a function with manual **width** and **height** argument.

- **position_dodge**(width, height)
- **position_fill**(width, height)
- **position_stack**(width, height)
- **position_jitter**(width, height)

```
p + geom_bar(position = position_dodge(width = 1))
```

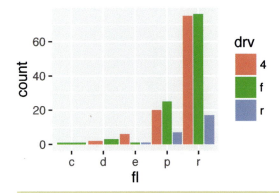

> See bar plots chapter: Chapter 20

Chapter 39

Coordinate Systems

```
p <- ggplot(mpg, aes(fl)) + geom_bar()
```

The **coordinate systems** in ggplot2 are:

- p + **coord_cartesian**(xlim = NULL, ylim = NULL): **Cartesian coordinate system** (default). It's the most familiar and common, type of coordinate system.

- p + **coord_fixed**(ratio = 1, xlim = NULL, ylim = NULL): **Cartesian coordinates with fixed relationship between x and y scales.** The ratio represents the number of units on the y-axis equivalent to one unit on the x-axis. The default, ratio = 1, ensures that one unit on the x-axis is the same length as one unit on the y-axis.

- p + **coord_flip**(...): **Flipped cartesian coordinates.** Useful for creating horizontal plot by rotating.

- p + **coord_polar**(theta = "x", start = 0, direction = 1): **Polar coordinates.** The polar coordinate system is most commonly used for pie charts, which are a stacked bar chart in polar coordinates.

- p + **coord_trans**(x, y, limx, limy): **Transformed cartesian coordinate system**.

- **coord_map**(): Map projections. Provides the full range of map projections available in the mapproj package.

1. Arguments for coord_cartesian(), coord_fixed() and coord_flip()

   - **xlim, ylim**: limits for the x and y axis, respectively
   - **ratio**: aspect ratio, expressed as y/x
   - **...**: Other arguments passed onto coord_cartesian

2. Arguments for coord_polar()

   - **theta**: variable to map angle to (x or y)
   - **start**: offset of starting point from 12 o'clock in radians
   - **direction**: 1, clockwise; -1, anticlockwise

3. Arguments for coord_trans()

   - **x, y**: transformers for x and y axes
   - **limx, limy**: limits for x and y axes.

```
p + coord_cartesian(ylim = c(0, 200)) # change y limits
p + coord_fixed(ratio = 1/50) # change ratio
p + coord_flip() # flip the plot
```

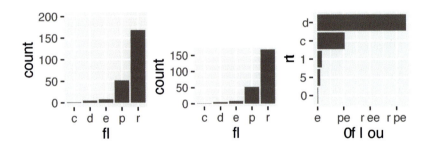

```
p + coord_polar(theta = "x", direction = 1)
p + coord_trans(y = "sqrt")
```

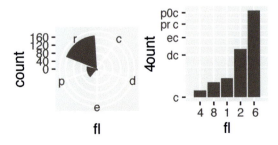

Part VI

Extensions to ggplot2

Chapter 40

Arrange Multiple Graphs on the Same Page

To arrange multiple ggplot2 graphs on the same page, the standard R functions - *par()* and *layout()* - cannot be used.

This chapter will show you, step by step, how to put several ggplots on a single page.

Key functions:

- **grid.arrange()**[in the package **gridExtra**]

- **plot_grid()** and **draw_plot()** [in the package **cowplot**]

40.1 Required R packages

The R packages **gridExtra** and **cowplot** are required.

1. **Installation:**

```
install.packages("gridExtra")
install.packages("cowplot")
```

2. **Loading**:

```r
library("gridExtra")
library("cowplot")
```

40.2   Data

ToothGrowth and *economics* data sets are used :

```r
# Load ToothGrowth
# Convert the variable dose from a numeric to a factor variable
data("ToothGrowth")
ToothGrowth$dose <- as.factor(ToothGrowth$dose)

data("economics") # Load economics
data("diamonds") # Load diamonds
```

40.3   cowplot: Arrange publication-ready plots

The **cowplot** package, developed by *Claus O. Wilke* provides a publication-ready theme for ggplot2 and allows to combine multiple plots in the same figure. We'll start by creating some plots, which will be combined using specific functions provided by the cowplot package.

40.3.1   Create some plots

We'll create series of 3 different plots:

- Box plot and dot plot using the *ToothGrowth* data set
- Line plot using the *economics* data set

We'll use custom colors to manually change line and fill colors (functions: *scale_color_manual()* and *scale_fill_manual()*; see Chapter 26)

- Define a custom set of 3 colors:

```r
# A set of 3 colors
my3cols <- c("#E7B800", "#2E9FDF", "#FC4E07")
```

- Create a box plot and a dot plot:

```r
require(cowplot)

p <- ggplot(ToothGrowth, aes(x = dose, y = len))

# Box plot (bp)
bxp <- p + geom_boxplot(aes(color = dose)) +
  scale_color_manual(values = my3cols)
bxp

# Dot plot (dp)
dp <- p + geom_dotplot(aes(color = dose, fill = dose),
                       binaxis='y', stackdir='center') +
  scale_color_manual(values = my3cols) +
  scale_fill_manual(values = my3cols)
dp
```

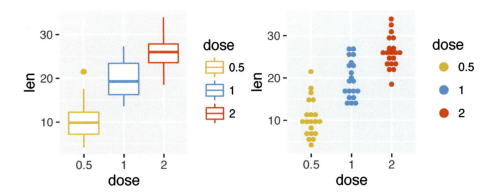

- Create a line plot:

```
lp <- ggplot(economics, aes(x = date, y = psavert)) +
  geom_line(color = "#E46726")
lp
```

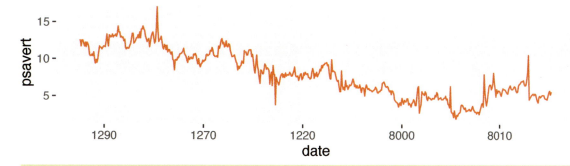

> Note that the default design of **cowplot** has white background with no grid at all.
> It looks similar to ggplot2's **theme_classic()**, but there are some subtle differences
> with respect to font sizes. In many cases, this is the cleanest and most elegant way
> to display the data.

If you want to add gridlines or to use the default ggplot2 theme, follow the R code
below:

```
# Add gridlines
bxp + background_grid(major = "xy", minor = "none")

# Use theme_gray()
bxp + theme_gray()
```

> The function *background_grid()* is from *cowplot* package.

40.3.2   Combine multiple plots

In this section we'll see how to combine the different plots created in the previous section.

Key functions:

- **plot_grid()**: Combines easily multiple plots

- **ggdraw() + draw_plot() + draw_plot_label()**: Place graphs at particular locations with a particular sizes.

In the R code below, the function **plot_grid()** is used to combine a box plot (bxp), a dot plot (dp) and a line plot (lp) on a grid of 2 columns and 2 rows:

```
plot_grid(bxp, dp, lp,  labels = c("A", "B", "C"),
          ncol = 2, nrow = 2)
```

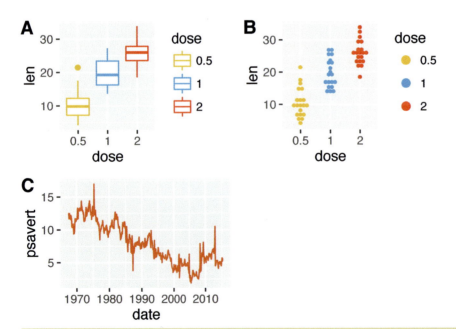

The combination of the functions **ggdraw()**, **draw_plot()** and **draw_plot_label()** can be used to place graphs and labels at particular locations with a particular sizes.

ggdraw(): Initialize an empty drawing canvas

draw_plot(): Places a plot somewhere onto the drawing canvas.

draw_plot_label(): Adds a plot label to the upper left corner of a graph. It can handle vectors of labels with associated coordinates.

- **Format of the function draw_plot():**

```
draw_plot(plot, x = 0, y = 0, width = 1, height = 1)
```

- **plot**: the plot to place (ggplot2 or a gtable)
- **x, y**: The x/y location of the lower left corner of the plot.
- **width, height**: the width and the height of the plot

Format of the function draw_plot_label():

```
draw_plot_label(label, x = 0, y = 1, size = 16, ...)
```

- **label**: a vector of labels to be drawn
- **x, y**: Vector containing the x and y position of the labels, respectively.
- **size**: Font size of the label to be drawn

Note that, by default, coordinates run from 0 to 1, and the point (0, 0) is in the lower left corner of the canvas (see the figure below).

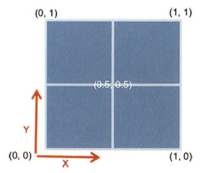

- Combine multiple plot with particular locations and different sizes:

```
ggdraw() +
  draw_plot(bxp, x = 0, y = .5, width = .5, height = .5) +
  draw_plot(dp, x = .5, y = .5, width = .5, height = .5) +
  draw_plot(lp, x = 0, y = 0, width = 1, height = 0.5) +
  draw_plot_label(label = c("A", "B", "C"),
                  x = c(0, 0.5, 0), y = c(1, 1, 0.5), size = 15)
```

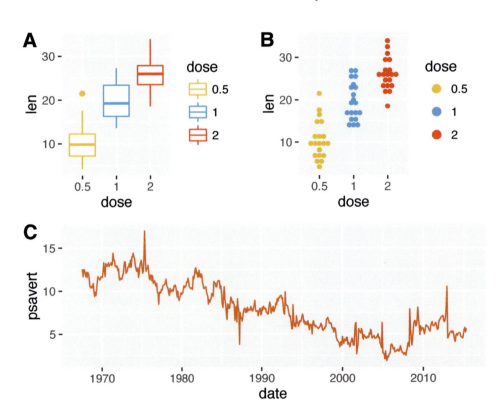

40.3.3   Save multi-figure plots

Recall that, the function **ggsave()**[in **ggplot2** package] (Chapter **??**) can be used to save ggplots. However, when working with **cowplot**, the function **save_plot()** [in **cowplot** package] is preferred.

> The cowplot default theme works nicely in conjunction with the save_plot(). The output pdfs are nicely formatted and scaled.

For example, if we want to save the box plot generated in the previous section, we might use this code:

```
# use save_plot() instead of ggsave() when using cowplot
save_plot("mpg.pdf", bxp,
          base_aspect_ratio = 1.3 # make room for figure legend
```

> The function **save_plot()** is also an alternative to **ggsave()** with a better support for multi-figure plots generated with **cowplot**. Furthermore, it can can be told about the grid layout.

For example, if we want to save a 2-by-2 figure, we might use this code:

```
plot2by2 <- plot_grid(bxp, dp, lp, labels = c("A", "B", "C"),
                      ncol = 2, nrow = 2)

save_plot("plot2by2.pdf", plot2by2,
          ncol = 2, # we're saving a grid plot of 2 columns
          nrow = 2, # and 2 rows
          # each individual subplot should have an aspect ratio of 1.3
          base_aspect_ratio = 1.3
          )
```

40.4 gridExtra package

40.4.1 grid.arrange(): Arrange multiple plots on a page

> The function **grid.arrange()**[in the package **gridExtra**] is another solution for mixing multiple graphs.

We'll combine the following plots:

- the box plot, the dot plot and the line plot created in the previous sections
- a bar plot created using the *diamonds* data sets as follow

```r
# Define a set of 5 colors
my5cols <- c("#6D9EC1", "#646567", "#A29B32", "#E46726", "#F3BF94")

# Create a bar plot
data("diamonds")
brp <- ggplot(diamonds, aes(x = clarity)) +
       geom_bar(aes(fill = cut)) + scale_fill_manual(values = my5cols)
```

Use **grid.arrange()** to combine the plot in a grid of 2 rows and 2 columns:

```r
require(gridExtra)
grid.arrange(bxp, dp, lp, brp, ncol = 2, nrow =2)
```

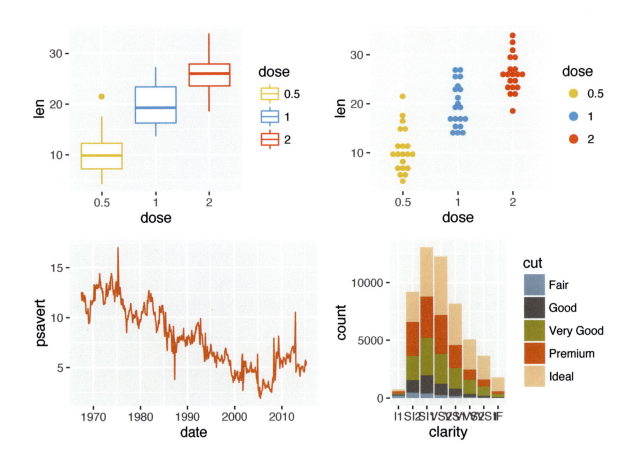

40.4.2 grid.arrange() and arrangeGrob(): Change column/row span of a plot

> The function **arangeGrop()** helps to change the row/column span of a plot.

For example, using the R code below:

- The box plot (bxp) will live in the first column
- The dot plot (dp) and the bar plot (brp) will live in the second column

```
grid.arrange(bxp, arrangeGrob(dp, brp), ncol = 2)
```

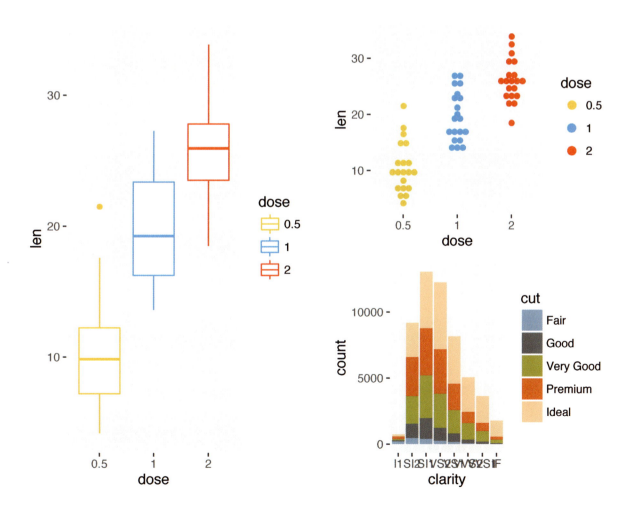

It's also possible to use the argument *layout_matrix* in grid.arrange() function.

In the R code below **layout_matrix** is a 2x2 matrix (2 columns and 2 rows). The first row is all 1s, that's where the first plot lives, spanning the three columns; the second row contains plots 2, 3, 4, each occupying one row.

```
grid.arrange(brp, bxp, dp, ncol = 2, nrow = 2,
             layout_matrix = rbind(c(1,1), c(2,3)))
```

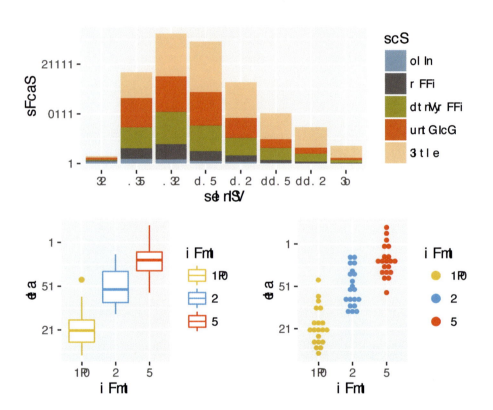

40.4.3   Use common legend for multiple graphs

This can be done in four simple steps :

1. Create the plots : p1, p2, ...
2. Save the legend of the plot p1 as an external graphical element (called a "grob" in Grid terminology)

3. Remove the legends from all plots
4. Draw all the plots with only one legend in the right panel

To **save the legend** of a ggplot, the helper function below can be used :

```
# Get plot legend
get_legend <- function(myggplot){
  require(gridExtra)
  tmp <- ggplot_gtable(ggplot_build(myggplot))
  leg <- which(sapply(tmp$grobs, function(x) x$name) == "guide-box")
  legend <- tmp$grobs[[leg]]
  return(legend)
}
```

We'll arrange the box plot (bxp) and the dot plot (dp) created in the previous sections.

```
# 2. Save the legend from the dot plot
legend <- get_legend(dp)

# 3. Remove the legend from the box plot and the dot plot
bxp2 <- bxp + theme(legend.position="none")
dp2 <- dp + theme(legend.position="none")

# 4. Arrange bxp2, dp and the legend with a specific width
grid.arrange(bxp2, dp2, legend, ncol = 3,
             widths = c(2.3, 2.3, 0.8))
```

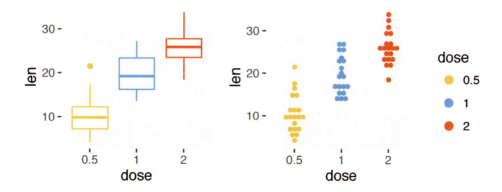

In the R code above, the argument **widths** is a vector containing 3 values specifying the width of the box plot (bxp2), the dot plot (dp2) and the legend, respectively.

It's also possible to use the argument **layout_matrix** to customize legend position. We start by creating a dot plot with a **top** legend position. Next, we save the legend and remove it from the dot plot:

```
# 1. Dot plot with legend at the top
dp2 <- dp + theme(legend.position = "top")

# 2. Save the legend
legend <- get_legend(dp2)

# 3. Remove the legend from the dot plot
dp2 <- dp2 + theme(legend.position = "none")
```

In the R code below, **layout_matrix** is a 2X2 matrix:

- The first row (height = 2.5) is where the first plot (bxp2) and the second plot (dp) live
- The second row (height = 0.2) is where the legend lives spanning 2 columns

Bottom-center legend:

```
grid.arrange(bxp2, dp2, legend, ncol=2, nrow = 2,
             layout_matrix = rbind(c(1,2), c(3,3)),
             widths = c(2.7, 2.7), heights = c(2.5, 0.2))
```

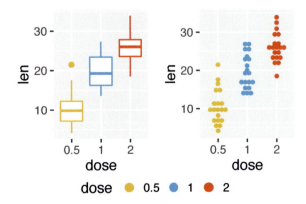

Top-center legend:

- The legend (plot 1) lives in the first row (height = 0.2) spanning two columns
- bxp2 (plot 2) and dp2 (plot 3) live in the second row (height = 2.5)

```
grid.arrange(legend, bxp2, dp2,  ncol=2, nrow = 2,
             layout_matrix = rbind(c(1,1), c(2,3)),
             widths = c(2.7, 2.7), heights = c(0.2, 2.5))
```

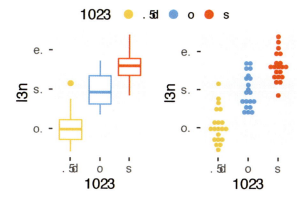

40.4.4   Scatter plot with marginal density plots

- **Define a custom set of 3 colors**:

```
# Another set of 3 colors
my3cols <- c("#6D9EC1", "#646567", "#A29B32")
```

Step 1/3. Create some data :

```
set.seed(1234)
x <- c(rnorm(350, mean = -1), rnorm(350, mean = 1.5),
       rnorm(350, mean = 4))

y <- c(rnorm(350, mean = -0.5), rnorm(350, mean = 1.7),
       rnorm(350, mean = 2.5))
```

```r
group <- as.factor(rep(c(1, 2, 3), each = 350))

df2 <- data.frame(x, y, group)
head(df2)
```

```
##              x              y group
## 1 -2.20706575 -0.715413865       1
## 2 -0.72257076 -0.009793331       1
## 3  0.08444118 -0.440606576       1
## 4 -3.34569770 -0.441687947       1
## 5 -0.57087531  1.338363107       1
## 6 -0.49394411 -0.112349101       1
```

Step 2/3. Create the plots:

```r
# Scatter plot of x and y variables and color by groups
scatterPlot <- ggplot(df2, aes(x, y)) +
  geom_point(aes(color = group)) +
  scale_color_manual(values = my3cols) +
  theme(legend.position=c(0,1), legend.justification=c(0,1))


# Marginal density plot of x (top panel)
xdensity <- ggplot(df2, aes(x)) +
  geom_density(aes(fill = group), alpha=.8) +
  scale_fill_manual(values = my3cols) +
  theme(legend.position = "none")

# Marginal density plot of y (right panel)
ydensity <- ggplot(df2, aes(y)) +
  geom_density(aes(fill=group), alpha=.8) +
  scale_fill_manual(values = my3cols) +
  theme(legend.position = "none") + coord_flip()
```

Create a blank placeholder plot :

```
blankPlot <- ggplot()+geom_blank(aes(1,1))+ theme_void()
```

Step 3/3. Put the plots together:

Arrange ggplot2 with adapted height and width for each row and column :

```
require("gridExtra")
grid.arrange(xdensity, blankPlot, scatterPlot, ydensity,
        ncol=2, nrow=2, widths=c(4, 1.4), heights=c(1.4, 4))
```

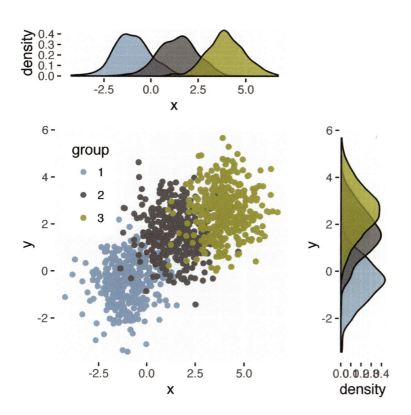

40.4.5   Create a complex layout using the function viewport()

The different steps are :

1. Create plots : p1, p2, p3, ...
2. Move to a new page on a grid device using the function **grid.newpage()**

3. Create a layout 2X2 - number of columns = 2; number of rows = 2
4. Define a grid viewport : a rectangular region on a graphics device
5. Print a plot into the viewport

```
require(grid)
# Move to a new page
grid.newpage()

# Create layout : nrow = 2, ncol = 2
pushViewport(viewport(layout = grid.layout(2, 2)))

# A helper function to define a region on the layout
define_region <- function(row, col){
  viewport(layout.pos.row = row, layout.pos.col = col)
}

# Arrange the plots
print(scatterPlot, vp=define_region(1, 1:2))
print(xdensity, vp = define_region(2, 1))
print(ydensity, vp = define_region(2, 2))
```

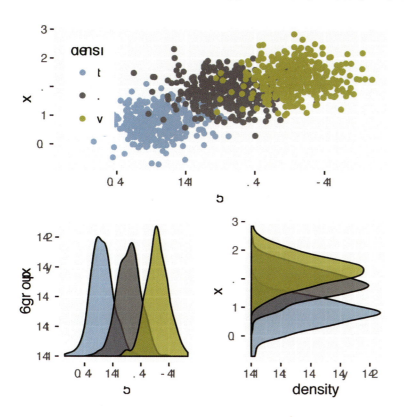

40.5   ggExtra: Add marginal distributions plots

The package **ggExtra** (https://github.com/daattali/ggExtra) is an easy-to-use package developed by Dean Attali, for adding marginal histograms, boxplots or density plots to ggplot2 scatter plots.

The package can be installed and used as follow:

```
# Install
install.packages("ggExtra")


library("ggExtra")

# Marginal density plot
ggMarginal(scatterPlot)
```

```
# Marginal histogram plot
ggMarginal(scatterPlot, type = "histogram",
           fill = "#6D9EC1", color = "#BFD5E3")
```

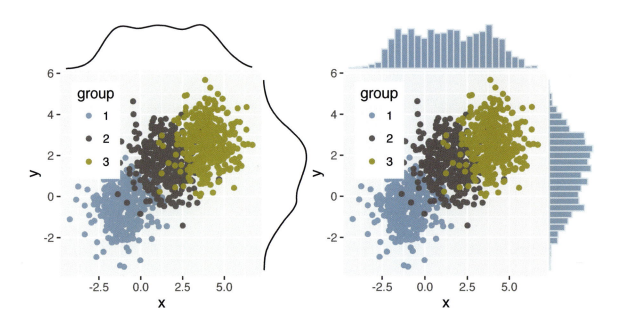

40.6   Insert an external graphical element inside a ggplot

The function **annotation_custom()** [in **ggplot2**] can be used for adding tables, plots or other grid-based elements. The simplified format is :

annotation_custom(grob, xmin, xmax, ymin, ymax)

- **grob**: the external graphical element to display
- **xmin, xmax** : x location in data coordinates (horizontal location)
- **ymin, ymax** : y location in data coordinates (vertical location)

The different steps are :

1. Create a scatter plot of y = f(x)

2. Add, for example, the box plot of the variables x and y inside the scatter plot using the function **annotation_custom()**

As the inset box plot overlaps with some points, a **transparent background** is used for the box plots.

```
# Create a transparent theme object
transparent_theme <- theme(
  axis.title.x = element_blank(),
  axis.title.y = element_blank(),
  axis.text.x = element_blank(),
  axis.text.y = element_blank(),
  axis.ticks = element_blank(),
  panel.grid = element_blank(),
  axis.line = element_blank(),
  panel.background = element_rect(fill = "transparent",colour = NA),
  plot.background = element_rect(fill = "transparent",colour = NA))
```

Create the graphs :

```
p1 <- scatterPlot # see previous sections for the scatterPlot

# Box plot of the x variable
p2 <- ggplot(df2, aes(factor(1), x))+
  geom_boxplot(width=0.3)+coord_flip()+
  transparent_theme

# Box plot of the y variable
p3 <- ggplot(df2, aes(factor(1), y))+
  geom_boxplot(width=0.3)+
  transparent_theme

# Create the external graphical elements
# called a "grop" in Grid terminology
p2_grob = ggplotGrob(p2)
p3_grob = ggplotGrob(p3)
```

```
# Insert p2_grob inside the scatter plot
xmin <- min(x); xmax <- max(x)
ymin <- min(y); ymax <- max(y)
p1 + annotation_custom(grob = p2_grob, xmin = xmin, xmax = xmax,
                       ymin = ymin-1.5, ymax = ymin+1.5)
```

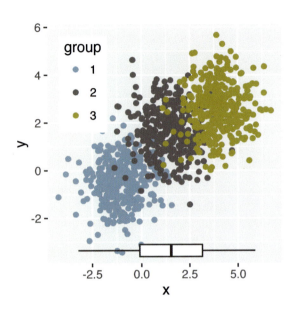

```
# Insert p3_grob inside the scatter plot
p1 + annotation_custom(grob = p3_grob,
                       xmin = xmin-1.5, xmax = xmin+1.5,
                       ymin = ymin, ymax = ymax)
```

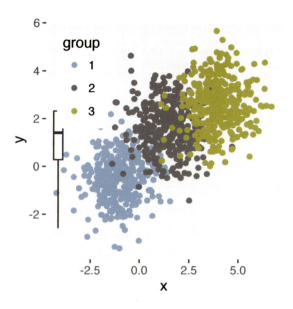

40.7   Mix table, text and ggplot2 graphs

The functions below are required :

- **tableGrob()** [in the package *gridExtra*] : for adding a data table to a graphic device
- **splitTextGrob()** [in the package *RGraphics*] : for adding a text to a graph

Make sure that the package **RGraphics** is installed.

```r
library(RGraphics)
library(gridExtra)

# Table
p1 <- tableGrob(head(ToothGrowth, 3))

# Text
text <- paste0("ToothGrowth data describes the effect ",
        "of Vitamin C on tooth growth in Guinea pigs.")
p2 <- splitTextGrob(text)
```

```r
# Box plot
p3 <- ggplot(ToothGrowth, aes(x = dose, y = len)) +
  geom_boxplot(aes(color = dose)) +
  scale_color_manual(values = my3cols)

# Arrange the plots on the same page
grid.arrange(p1, p2, p3, ncol=1,
             heights = c(0.25, 0.2, 0.55))
```

	len	supp	dose
1	4.2	VC	0.5
2	11.5	VC	0.5
3	7.3	VC	0.5

ToothGrowth data describes the effect of Vitamin C on tooth growth in Guinea pigs.

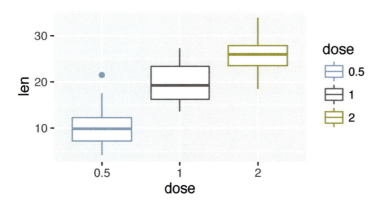

Chapter 41

Correlation Matrix Visualization

The R packages **GGally** and **ggcorrplot** are two extensions to ggplot2 for displaying a correlation matrix.

Compared to **GGally**, the **ggcorrplot** package provides many options for visualizing a correlation matrix. For example, it provides a solution for reordering the correlation matrix and displays the significance level on the correlogram. It includes also a function for computing a matrix of correlation p-values.

41.1 GGally

Compute and visualize a correlation matrix:

```
# Correlation matrix
library("GGally")
mydata <- mtcars[, c(1,3,4,5,6,7)]
ggcorr(mydata, palette = "RdBu", label = TRUE)
```

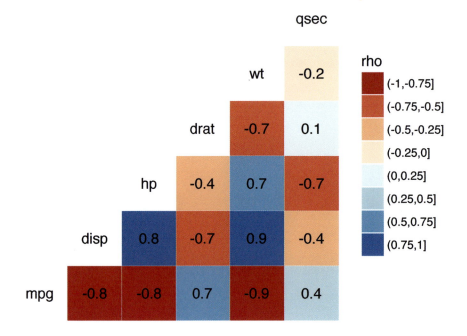

```
# Matrix of scatter plot
ggpairs(mydata)
```

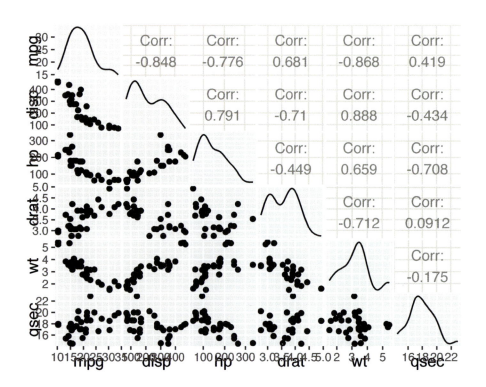

41.2   ggcorrplot

41.2.1   Installation and loading

ggcorrplot can be installed from CRAN as follow:

```r
install.packages("ggcorrplot")
```

Or, install the latest version from GitHub:

```r
# Install
if(!require(devtools)) install.packages("devtools")
devtools::install_github("kassambara/ggcorrplot")
```

41.2.2   Compute a correlation matrix

```r
library("ggcorrplot")
# Compute a correlation matrix
mydata <- mtcars[, c(1,3,4,5,6,7)]
corr <- round(cor(mydata), 1)
head(corr[, 1:6], 3)
```

```
##       mpg disp   hp drat   wt qsec
## mpg   1.0 -0.8 -0.8  0.7 -0.9  0.4
## disp -0.8  1.0  0.8 -0.7  0.9 -0.4
## hp   -0.8  0.8  1.0 -0.4  0.7 -0.7
```

```r
# Compute a matrix of correlation p-values
p.mat <- cor_pmat(mydata)
head(p.mat[, 1:4], 3)
```

```
##               mpg         disp           hp         drat
## mpg  0.000000e+00 9.380327e-10 1.787835e-07 1.776240e-05
## disp 9.380327e-10 0.000000e+00 7.142679e-08 5.282022e-06
## hp   1.787835e-07 7.142679e-08 0.000000e+00 9.988772e-03
```

41.2.3   Correlation matrix visualization

```
# Visualize the correlation matrix
# --------------------------------
# method = "square" (default)
ggcorrplot(corr)

# Reordering the correlation matrix
# --------------------------------
# using hierarchical clustering
ggcorrplot(corr, hc.order = TRUE, outline.col = "white")
```

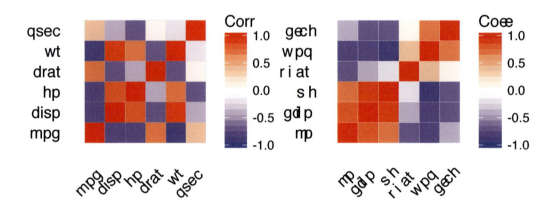

```
# Types of correlogram layout and customization
# --------------------------------
# Add correlation coefficients
ggcorrplot(corr, hc.order = TRUE,
   type = "lower", # get the lower triangle
   outline.col = "white",
   ggtheme = ggplot2::theme_bw, # change theme
   colors = c("#6D9EC1", "white", "#E46726"), # change color palette
   lab = TRUE # Add correlation coefficients
   )


# Add correlation significance level
# --------------------------------
```

```
# Argument p.mat
# Barring the no significant coefficient
ggcorrplot(corr, hc.order = TRUE,
    type = "lower", p.mat = p.mat)
```

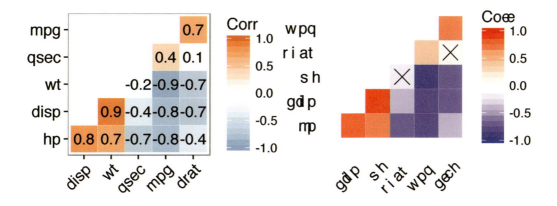

Chapter 42

Plotting Survival Curves

Survival analysis focuses on the expected duration of time until occurrence of an event of interest. However, this failure time may not be observed within the study time period, producing the so-called **censored** observations.

The R package **survival** fits and plots survival curves using R base graphs.

Here, we developed and present the **survminer** R package for drawing survival curves using ggplot2 system.

42.1   Fitting survival curves

1. The R package **survival** is required. It can be installed as follow:

```
install.packages("survival")
```

2. **Data set**: *lung* data set from **survival** package:

```
data(lung, package = "survival")
# head(lung)
```

The data above includes:

- time: Survival time in days
- status: censoring status $1 = $ censored, $2 = $ dead
- sex: Male $= 1$; Female $= 2$

3. **Fitting survival curves**

```
library("survival")
fit <- survfit(Surv(time, status) ~ sex, data = lung)
```

42.2   Drawing survival curves with survminer

The R package **survminer** contains the function **ggsurvplot()** for easily drawing beautiful and ready-to-publish survival curves using **ggplot2**. **ggsurvplot()** includes also some options for displaying the **p-value** and the **'number at risk' table**, under the survival curves. survminer can be installed either from CRAN or GitHub.

- Install from CRAN:

```
install.packages(survminer)
```

- Install the latest version of survminer from GitHub:

```
if(!require(devtools)) install.packages("devtools")
devtools::install_github("kassambara/survminer")
```

- Loading

```
library("survminer")
```

42.2.1   ggsurvplot: Drawing survival curves

42.2.1.1   Basic plots

```
# Drawing survival curves
ggsurvplot(fit)
```

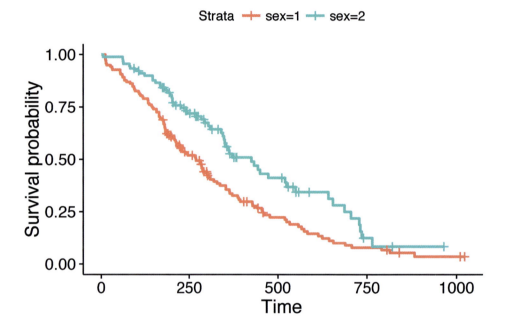

42.2.1.2   Customize survival curves

```
ggsurvplot(fit,  size = 1,  # change line size
          palette = c("#E7B800", "#2E9FDF"), # custom color palette
          conf.int = TRUE, # Add confidence interval
          pval = TRUE, # Add p-value
          risk.table = TRUE, # Add risk table
          risk.table.col = "strata", # Risk table color by groups
          ggtheme = theme_bw() # Change ggplot2 theme
          )
```

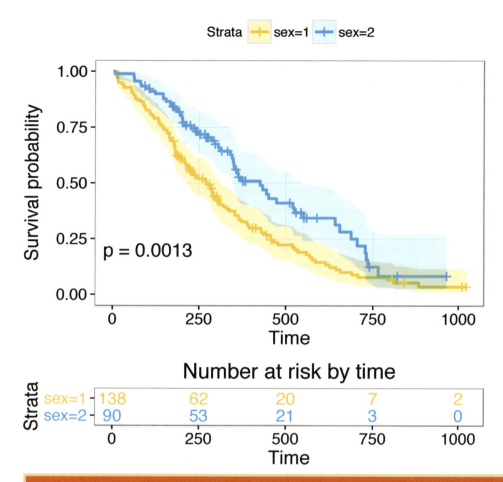

Note that, allowed values, for the argument **palette**, include "hue" for the default hue color scale; "grey" for grey color palettes; brewer palettes e.g. "RdBu", "Blues", "Dark2", ...; or custom color palette e.g. c("blue", "red").

Other useful arguments are also available in ggsurvplot (see ?ggsurvplot).

Chapter 43

References and further reading

43.1 Extensions to ggplot2: R packages and functions

- factoextra: **factoextra : Extract and Visualize the outputs of a multivariate analysis**. **factoextra** provides some easy-to-use functions to extract and visualize the output of PCA (Principal Component Analysis), CA (Correspondence Analysis) and MCA (Multiple Correspondence Analysis) functions from several packages (FactoMineR, stats, ade4 and MASS). It contains also many functions for simplifying clustering analysis workflows. Ggplot2 plotting system is used.

- ggfortify: Define **fortify** and **autoplot** functions to allow ggplot2 to handle some popular R packages. These include plotting 1) Matrix; 2) Linear Model and Generalized Linear Model; 3) Time Series; 4) PCA/Clustering; 5) Survival Curve; 6) Probability distribution

- GGally: **GGally** extends ggplot2 by providing several functions including **pairwise correlation matrix**, **scatterplot plot matrix**, **parallel coordinates plot**, **survival plot** and several functions to plot networks.

- ggRandomForests: Graphical analysis of **random forests** with the randomForestSRC and ggplot2 packages.

- ggdendro: Create dendrograms and tree diagrams using ggplot2

- ggmcmc: Tools for Analyzing MCMC Simulations from Bayesian Inference

- ggthemes: Package with additional ggplot2 themes and scales

43.2 Cheat Sheets

- Be Awesome in ggplot2: A Practical Guide to be Highly Effective
- Data Visualization with ggplot2, RStudio cheat sheet
- Beautiful plotting in R: A ggplot2 cheatsheet

43.3 References

This book was written in R Markdown inside RStudio. knitr and pandoc converted the raw Rmarkdown to pdf. This version of the book was built with **R** (ver. x86_64-apple-darwin13.4.0, x86_64, darwin13.4.0, x86_64, darwin13.4.0, , 3, 2.3, 2015, 12, 10, 69752, R, R version 3.2.3 (2015-12-10), Wooden Christmas-Tree), **ggplot2** (ver. 2.1.0) and **dplyr** (ver. 0.4.3)

- Hadley Wickman. Elegant graphics for data analysis. Springer 2009. http://ggplot2.org/book/
- Hadley Wickman. ggplot2 official documentation. http://docs.ggplot2.org/current/
- Winston Chang. R graphics cookbook. O'Reilly 2012. http://www.cookbook-r.com/
- Alboukadel Kassambara. Data analysis and visualization. http://www.sthda.com/english/wiki/ggplot2-introduction

17182333R00141

Printed in Poland
by Amazon Fulfillment
Poland Sp. z o.o., Wrocław